MW00648983

MARY IN THE BIBLE
AND IN OUR LIVES

WILFRID STINISSEN, O.C.D.

Mary in the Bible and in Our Lives

~

Translated by
Sister Clare Marie, O.C.D.

IGNATIUS PRESS   SAN FRANCISCO

From the third edition of the Swedish original:
Maria i Biblen—i vårt liv
© 1999 by Karmeliterna, Tågarp

Cover art:
Last Judgement, detail of the Virgin Mary
Pietro Cavallini (c. 1250–1330)
S. Cecilia in Trastevere, Rome, Italy
© Scala/Art Resource, New York

Cover design by Roxanne Mei Lum

© 2018 by Ignatius Press, San Francisco
All rights reserved
ISBN 978-1-62164-187-2
Library of Congress Control Number 2017941602
Printed in the United States of America ∞

Contents

1. "Without Spot or Wrinkle" 9

   Why This Privilege? 9
   An Absolute Yes 11
   The Perfect Human Being 13
   A Lack of Solidarity? 16
   The Teaching of the Church 18

2. "Be It Done to Me according to Your
   Word". 21

   The Father 22
   The Son 23
   The Spirit 25
   Mary's Response 26
   A Yes to Both God and Man 29
   The Angelus. 29

3. Mary Visits Elizabeth 31

   Why This Visit? 31
   A Living Monstrance. 33
   Jesus Meets John 34
   *Mary and Elizabeth Awaken the Spirit in
   Each Other* 36

4. Mary and Joseph 39

   "Mary Was Engaged to Joseph". 40
   Joseph's Reaction 41

The Virgin Birth a Myth? 43
Ever Virgin 46

5. Mother of God 49

Mary's Advent 49
Theotokos 50
The Mother of God for the Sake of the World 54

6. Jesus Is Presented in the Temple 57

"For Their Sake I Consecrate Myself"
  (John 17:19) 57
The Dialogue between Mary and Simeon 59

7. Jesus Is Lost in the Temple 65

The Identity of Jesus 66
"I Sought Him" 67
"Why?" 68
The Holy Family 70

8. Mary at Cana 73

"The Mother of Jesus Was There" 73
Mary's Prayer 74
"Woman" 77
Jesus' Hour 78
Mother of Good Counsel 79
A Crescendo 81

9. Mary at the Foot of the Cross 83

The New Eve 83
"A Fitting Helper for Him" 86
Mother of the Church 87

Contents

10. Mary and the Holy Spirit 93

   The "Motherly" Mission of the Spirit and
      Mary 94
   Mary's Pentecost 97
   Mary and Peter 100

11. The Assumption of Mary 103

   Taken up into Heaven 104
   A New Presence 106
   The Church's Assumption 107
   The Dogma Defined 110

12. Mary and the Church 113

   A Masculine Church? 114
   Mary, Archetype of the Church 115
   The Church Is Characterized by Mary 118
   An Open Church 121

13. Our Lady of the Dark Night 125

   To Die in Order to Live 125
   Mary's Dark Night 127
   "Who Is My Mother?" 129
   Star of the Sea 132
   Mary Mediates God's "Motherly" Love 135

14. The Marian Cult 137

   Mary's Unique Position 138
   Through Mary 140
   With Mary 144
   In Mary 149

15. The Rosary. 155

    Vocal Prayer. 155
    Meditative Prayer 156
    Contemplative Prayer. 159
    Intercession. 160
    The Prayer of Poverty. 161
    Family Prayer 162

Appendix 1: The Angelus. 165

Appendix 2: The Mysteries of the Rosary. 167

I

"Without Spot or Wrinkle"

When we speak of the Immaculate Conception of the Blessed Virgin Mary, many, even among Catholics, think of the conception of Christ that occurred in Mary's womb without harm to her virginity through a special intervention of the Holy Spirit. The Immaculate Conception of Mary is also truly a work of the Holy Spirit, but a work that took place in her at the very moment she came into being. Mary was free from original sin from the first moment of her existence. She was spared the contagion of the original sin that affects all of mankind. From the very beginning she was completely free of guilt.

Why This Privilege?

Let us first point out that the word "privilege" is not really fitting in this case. "Privilege" is related to "private". The more privileges a person receives, the more he takes an exceptional position and distinguishes himself from others. But what Mary received, she received for others. Self-glorification was completely foreign to Mary. She never desired to be greater than others, as many of us do. That is why theologians have often done her a disservice by adorning her with every possible privilege, making her an extremely exalted creature with whom one can no longer have any human relationship.

The liturgical texts used by the Church on the Solemnity of the Immaculate Conception (December 8) clearly express why Mary was preserved from the guilt of original sin and all other sin. The Church says to the Father: "O God, who by the Immaculate Conception of the Blessed Virgin prepared a worthy dwelling for your Son" (Collect). Mary was predestined to be the Mother of God. God chose her to give birth, by the power of the Holy Spirit, to a child who was God's own Son, indeed like us in all things but "without sinning" (Heb 4:15). How could she have been a worthy partner of the Holy Spirit and given birth to an "immaculate" Son if she herself had not been without sin? God willed that Jesus would receive from her everything a child normally receives from his mother: not merely his physical body, but also his hereditary disposition, his temperament, his whole psyche. It was part of God's plan that the Son would receive his life unconditionally from his Mother: nothing in her would be rejected, nothing excluded. Mary was so holy through and through that she could give herself totally to her child. Any other arrangement would have created a distance between Mother and Son, a distance that could have implied that God did not accept all the consequences of being human.

The liturgy also says Mary was preserved from sin "so that in her, endowed with the rich fullness of your grace, you might prepare a worthy Mother for your Son and signify the beginning of the Church, his beautiful Bride without spot or wrinkle" (preface). Mary is not only the Mother of Jesus. When she stood at the foot of the Cross, she became the New Eve. There she stood in a bridal relationship to the New Adam. The Church that God sees as the Bride of Christ (cf. 2 Cor 11:2, Eph 5:23ff.) is not only a collection of individuals. She is embodied in a concrete, living person. When Jesus gave himself on the Cross, the Church was not absent, she was present in Mary. If Mary had not been immaculate, she could never have been an image of the Church, the pure Virgin, "without spot or wrinkle" (Eph 5:27).

An Absolute Yes

That Mary was free from original sin means, in essence, that she did not have to struggle with an innate egoism as we do. She was totally open to God from the beginning. From the first moment of her existence she stood directly under God, with mouth open wide (cf. Ps 81:10). Therefore, not a moment of her life was lost. She did not lose a single gift God had planned for her. She let herself be entirely penetrated, like a sponge that absorbs water but is never saturated. In her there was no resistance to love. *We* usually put up a fight with God, a fight that, for most of us, ends only at death, that wonderful invention of God that finally forces us to surrender to him.[1] With Mary, surrender was an obvious fact from the moment she came into being. She lived in an absolute obedience. She was a "handmaid of the Lord" from the beginning, who was never enticed to stray from being at God's disposal. When Saint Thérèse of Lisieux (1873–1897) writes that she never refused God anything from the time she was three years old, she means that she never said a conscious No to God.[2] But in reality, Thérèse, without knowing it, often gave in to a certain self-centeredness. Her conscious Yes could not have been without many small, unconscious Nos. Mary's Yes, on the other hand, filled not only her consciousness, but her entire being. She was a living "Yes, Father." Her Yes poured forth spontaneously from her unconscious. She did not need to force it, because saying Yes was her life.

The more Mary said Yes, the greater her inner capacity grew. We can imagine she felt a particular joy when she prayed or heard the Psalm verse "you have opened my heart." God predestined her to say a Yes that would be the response of all mankind to his in-

[1] Cf. Adrienne von Speyr, "Death is God's invention that finally prevents the sinner from resisting His grace", in *Lumina and New Lumina*, trans. Adrian Walker (San Francisco: Ignatius Press, 2008), 59.

[2] Saint Thérèse of Lisieux, *Her Last Conversations*, trans. John Clarke, O.C.D. (Washington, D.C.: ICS Publications, Institute of Carmelite Studies, 1977), 251.

vitation. God respects man's freedom in his relationship with him. Again and again, God made a covenant with man. He considered him a genuine partner in his covenant. When the moment of the Incarnation arrived, and God wished to say his final Yes to man, he wanted to give him the possibility of responding with a Yes that was equally definitive and unconditional. No sinful human being is capable of such a response, but Mary was prepared for it by this Yes-disposition that had been imprinted in her being from the beginning. With her created, but no less absolute, Yes, God's divine Yes could enter into a marriage, the fruit of which would be Jesus, the Savior of the world. Just as God's Yes concerned all mankind, so Mary's Yes was received as the response of all mankind.

The Perfect Human Being

While we readily flee into abstractions, it seems nothing lies nearer to God's heart than being concrete. The Incarnation is almost a frightening proof of that. It is easier for us to accept an abstract, distant, and thus harmless God than a God who comes close to us and who through concrete, unambiguous actions shows us how he is and how we can follow him. We have an incurable tendency to transform the concrete ideal into ideologies. God, on the other hand, knows that reality is never abstract. That is why he does not allow man to strive for abstract goals that are attained only when the full development process is finished. He usually gives us a concrete image of the goal at the beginning of the journey. Before we start off, we are allowed to behold and often even experience something of what we shall receive at the end of our journey. Aristotle's principle, that the goal is the first thing one holds in one's mind, even if it is the final reality, is only a watered down version of God's principle, according to which the goal is there from the beginning, not only as an intention, but to a certain degree also as a concrete reality. When Jesus warns us: "Unless you turn and become like children, you will never enter the kingdom of heaven" (Mt 18:3), we all understand what he means. As children, we have experienced a condition of complete dependency and total surrender. This condition must be recaptured, but now consciously and freely. When depth psychology claims that man unconsciously longs to return to the original security of the mother's womb, it reveals something of the pedagogy of the Creator. The last is always first. The last is anticipated in the first, so that we will have certain, clear reference points on the long journey toward the goal.

Is there need for more examples? In the prayer life of an individual it seems to be a general rule in the beginning to be flooded with joy: that final peace which passes all understanding is given already as a first hint. The same thing happens when one crosses over the threshold of mysticism into the prayer of quiet (the fourth dwelling place, or "mansion", in Saint Teresa of Avila's Interior Castle) and experiences how he is filled with "heavenly water" and penetrated by a "fragrant perfume".[3] One is able to experience in a transitory and more peripheral way even here what becomes a definitive reality in total union (the sixth mansion): "It is no longer I who live, but Christ who lives in me" (Gal 2:20).

What applies to every individual person applies also to all mankind. When God begins his work of recreation and desires to replace the old order of things, which had degenerated into a "Sein zum Tode" (being toward death) (Heidegger) due to the Fall, he first creates, with a new dynamic, a person who realizes the ideal in a perfect way, an ideal all people will strive to follow in the future. God's dream is incarnated in Mary. Jesus is, of course, a perfect human being, but he stands, first of all, on the side of God. He is Emmanuel, "God with us". Mary is "the human being with God". It must be clear for all from the beginning what a human being is when she is "with God". The goal of what mankind is called to be is an accomplished fact in Mary. In her, paradise has been restored on earth. In her, God's dream of mankind has become a concrete reality.

How could Mary be without sin before Jesus had saved the world? Did Mary not need salvation? Is she the only person Jesus did not need to die for on the Cross? No, Mary is in truth the most wonderful fruit of

---

[3] *The Interior Castle* IV, 2, 6, in *The Collected Works of Saint Teresa of Avila*, vol. 2, trans. Kieran Kavanaugh, O.C.D., and Otilio Rodrigues, O.C.D. (Washington, D.C.: Institute of Carmelite Studies, 1980), 324.

Christ's suffering. The Church has always known that
it was "by virtue of the Death of your Son" (Church
prayer) that God preserved Mary from all stain of guilt.
She was a gift that the Father prepared for the Son beforehand when he came into the world. The Father
wanted to show the Son that the way he had chosen
to walk was the right way. Yes, it was shown from the
beginning that the way of the Cross would lead to the
goal, in that it could bear a fruit as fully ripe as Mary.
Jesus had only to look at his Mother to be convinced
that his suffering would not be in vain.

A Lack of Solidarity?

Some object that Mary's Immaculate Conception re-
moves her from the rest of humanity. How can we
consider her to be one of us when we know something as typical as sin and guilt are completely foreign
to her?

But does sin really create solidarity? Does sin not
rather alienate us from each other? In hell there is no
solidarity, only terrible loneliness. The root of sin,
which is egoism, makes it difficult for man to open
himself to others. The biographies of the saints bear
witness to the immense capacity for solidarity received
by those who have been purified. The one who is no
longer interested in himself can be completely engaged
in the suffering and needs of others. We can only speak
about taking on the guilt of others when we have been
to some degree purified. It is Mary's total purity that

makes a total solidarity possible in her. That some have hesitated for so long to ascribe to Mary a total freedom from sin is surely due to a lack of understanding that it is precisely sin that isolates people. To be sure, there is something we can call the communion of sinners or solidarity in sin, but the reason such a communion exists is because certain "sinners" have distanced themselves from sin, thus opening themselves enough to take part in the misery of their fellowmen.

We often tend to see a kind of antagonism between holiness and humanity. When we hear about the mistakes of others, we think: "That is human." Though such a reaction may spring from love, it can easily contribute to the idea that "humanity" is associated with sin. If we are completely consistent in this, we might draw the conclusion that Jesus was not truly man (Docetism). Is it not the exact opposite? Is Jesus not the true human being, and does man not become more human in the measure he comes closer to him? Sin is something "inhuman", and therefore it will not be found in heaven, for as Saint Ignatius of Antioch writes: "When I have gone [from this world], I shall indeed be a man of God."[4] In his book *Mary, Mother of the Lord*, Max Thurian wonders if the Reformation's resistance to Mary's sinlessness and its reaction to asceticism and the monastic life are not related. In both cases it can be a question of a naturalist concept of the Christian life that regards asceticism, contemplation,

---

[4] *Letter to the Romans*, no. 6.

and striving for holiness as an escape from the "normal" relationships of human nature.[5]

The Teaching of the Church

On December 8, 1854, Pius IX solemnly declared the Immaculate Conception of Mary to be a truth revealed by God. He referred, among other things, to Luke 1:28, where the angel greets Mary: "Hail, full of grace." This was not an ordinary greeting. It was rather a title, one could even say a personal name, that expressed Mary's being. The perfect tense in the original Greek text (*kecharitoménē*) alludes to a fact in the past: Mary did not become full of grace at the moment she was greeted by the angel. It was a part of her very being to be full of grace. And she received this fullness from the beginning, in light of that moment when she would receive through the angel Gabriel the message that she was chosen to be the Mother of God.

It is obvious that this radical interpretation of Saint Luke's text can only be accepted by those who believe that Scripture was given to the Church and that the Church alone can guarantee the interpretation and explanation of Scripture without deviating from the truth. The words "full of grace" themselves do not necessarily mean that Mary was preserved from all sin. But it was the mission of the Church, under the guid-

[5] Max Thurian, *Mary, Mother of the Lord*, trans. Neville B. Cryer (London: Faith Press, 1963), 23–24.

ance of the Holy Spirit, to discover eventually what God had in fact meant when through the angel he gave Mary this exceptional name.

Four years after the declaration of the dogma on March 25, 1858, the beautiful Lady at Lourdes revealed her name. It was surely no accident that it happened on the feast of the Annunciation. She had already appeared to the fourteen-year-old girl Bernadette fifteen times without disclosing her identity. But this last time the answer came: "Que soy era Immaculada Councepciou" (I am the Immaculate Conception). Despite the fact that the beautiful Lady spoke her dialect, Bernadette did not understand the meaning of the words. It did not even occur to her that this could be a name for Mary, which made the message from heaven all the more convincing. Mary herself confirmed the name the Church had given to her four years earlier. We can understand why Pastor Peyramal, who always showed skepticism toward Bernadette's alleged visions, finally capitulated. When he heard Bernadette pronounce these words, which for her were incomprehensible—on the way to the rectory she had repeated them uninterruptedly—he burst into tears.

2

"Be It Done to Me according to Your Word"

The New Covenant begins at the Annunciation. The dialogue between the angel and Mary presented by Saint Luke (1:26–38) is without doubt the most important dialogue that has ever taken place. The entire Old Covenant is a preparation for this conversation, and the New Covenant has been made possible only by Mary's Yes in this dialogue. Who could comprehend that God would lay such an immense responsibility on one single person?

The angel speaks in God's name; Mary represents mankind. In reality, this is a conversation between God and man and a prototype of every conversation between heaven and earth. Mary is the great example for every believing person. This conversation can also teach us how we should converse with God.

When we read this dialogue attentively, we see that it consists of three parts. This is not unusual, since it is God who is the principal partner in the dialogue, and God is triune. If one listens carefully to the angel, one comes to know more about God's inner life. The three divine Persons come forth successively in the dialogue's three phases. It is the first time God speaks in this way, the first time he reveals himself so clearly as Trinity.

The Father

The initiative comes from God. It is he who begins the dialogue through the angel. "Hail, full of grace!" the angel says to Mary, "The Lord is with you." The Lord is the Father. Everything has its origin in him. Unexpectedly he lets himself be known. The angel does not knock on the door. Mary has no time to prepare herself. Suddenly the angel is there. Without invitation, he comes to greet her. Later Jesus would also say that the Son of Man shall come like a thief in the night (Mt 24:43–44). When God intervenes, it almost always happens at an unexpected moment, when one is least thinking of it. He does not announce himself beforehand; he wants us to be ready, awake with loins girt (Lk 12:35).

When God steps into her life, Mary's first reaction is fright: "She was greatly troubled." God's presence is overwhelming, and it makes its demands. He places man before something new, something of which he has no grasp, an adventure that involves risks. She must leave her old life and habits behind and say farewell to old familiar customs. When God breaks into our world, it always entails a breaking out of *our* world. This makes us anxious.

"[Mary] considered in her mind what sort of greeting this might be", Saint Luke adds. He emphasizes in his Gospel that Mary pondered. She reflected. She let the angel's words sink down into her heart. Reflection of this kind is not very common in our day. We often run about here and there and have no time to listen to God. There are so many other more meaningful things that are pressing. We must make plans in both the long and the short term, but unfortunately almost never in view of eternity. We see only a fragment of the road, but not where it is leading, what the goal is and the meaning of life.

The Son

Then comes the second phase of the dialogue. "Do not be afraid, Mary", God says through the angel. He now calls Mary by name. God does not love us collectively. He loves each one individually. Each one of us is irreplaceable. God is an artist who does not repeat himself, who does not plagiarize. No leaf is like another, nor is any fingerprint or soul. When God turns to man, he prefers to speak in the singular: You.

"Behold," says the angel, "you will conceive in your womb and bear a son, and you shall call his name Jesus. He will be great and will be called the Son of the Most High." Here the second Person of the Trinity enters in. The Son, who has already said his Yes to the Father within the Trinity, is prepared to become man. This is incomprehensible. God wills to become man in the womb of this Jewish girl. Man does not need to struggle with great effort to get to heaven; heaven itself comes to earth. Every time God speaks to man, it always amounts to this in the end: he wishes to come and make his dwelling in him. Naturally Mary's place in salvation history is unique: she becomes the Mother of God. But Jesus himself says that we can, to a certain degree, imitate her in this: "My mother and my brethren are those who hear the word of God and do it" (Lk 8:21).

When Mary speaks for the first time in this dialogue, her answer is a question. We are perhaps surprised at this. Mary's first word is not Yes, not Amen, but a question.

Now there are many ways of asking a question. Saint Luke is aware of this, and for that very reason he discreetly alludes to Zechariah's "annunciation". The decisive moment in both annunciations is the first reaction of these two people, their first answer. In both instances the answer appears to be an objection. But it is the similarity that makes the difference more clear. Let us look at them. Mary's response is: "How can this be?", Zechariah's response is: "How shall I know this?" Mary's words and thoughts are about *this*, Zechariah's, on the other hand, are about *me*. Zechariah thinks about himself, about his own insufficient certainty; he would like to have a sign. His egocentric way of asking interrupts the dialogue and leads to muteness. Mary does not do this. Her answer is a rather down-to-earth, practical question that would be typical for a woman. Beneath the negative surface of the question, she goes to the heart of the matter. She asks about what she concretely must do. Saint Paul did the same when he was thrown off his horse on the way to Damascus: "Lord, what would you have me do?" (Acts 9:6, Vulgate). There is always the danger that we are living in our pious dreams, because we do not let God's demands take concrete form. It is nice to dream about holiness and perfection, but as long as we do not understand what this obliges us to do in everyday, concrete reality, nothing has happened with us yet. Mary asks concretely and soberly how she shall conduct herself in relationship to Joseph.

The Spirit

In the third phase of the dialogue, the angel answers Mary's question: "The Holy Spirit will come upon you, and the power of the Most High will overshadow you." Now the third Person of the Trinity enters in. What shall come to pass is not the fruit of human effort. The Spirit will accomplish it. God must give his power in order for the promise to become reality. And he *wants* to give it, he *will* give it.

"For with God nothing will be impossible." God usually gives man a mission that is impossible for him to fulfill himself. In this way he lets him see that he is not enough and that only one thing remains: a boundless trust in him. "Commit your way to the LORD; trust in him, and he will act" (Ps 37:5). No one ever received a mission as impossible as Mary's. That a human being could give birth to God's Son is something that seems possible only in myths and fairy tales. But neither has anyone been able to experience as clearly as Mary did that God does not abandon man. Her capacity for the infinite increased when he allowed her to come under the shadow of his Spirit.

Mary's Response

Now everything was clear to Mary. She understood God's invitation. The last word must come from her. It was on this word that everything depended. All of history had been waiting for this word, ever since the Fall of Adam. God spoke to man even earlier, but never really received an answer. Perhaps one could say the meaning of the Old Covenant was that God wanted to prepare his people little by little until they were finally in a position to bring forth someone who could give him an adequate response. Mary spoke that decisive word in the name of all mankind: "Behold, I am the handmaid of the Lord; let it be to me according to your word." God's word and Mary's word became one, they coincided. For the first time since the Fall of man, a total agreement reigned between heaven and earth, exactly as it had at the act of creation. "And God said, 'Let there be light'; and there was light" (Gen 1:3). You shall be Mother to my Son, God says. "Let it be", Mary responded. With absolute clarity God invited, and the answer was: Let it be done! There is not much to analyze or brood over. The answer is always the same: Yes. "Come", says the bridegroom. "Yes, I am coming", answers the bride.

Mary's great Yes included and encompassed all our small Yeses. Our Yes would hardly have any meaning if Mary's Yes had not been there first. Her Yes anticipated and contains all the Yeses that would come after her. She did as a godparent does at baptism who responds to all the questions in the name of the child. But the original Yes must then be confirmed and owned in the child's life, in our lives.

The greatest word that a human being has ever uttered is amazingly simple. Our first reaction when we hear this word is perhaps: "Is that all?" Yes, that is all! Mary said Yes to God. She let God be God. God wanted to love her and, in her, all of mankind. She answered, and, in her, all mankind answered: "Love me." God wanted to fill her hands, and she stretched out her empty hands and let them be filled. She gave Love the chance to be realized.

Mary's Yes is only an echo of God's original Yes, if we look at it in its deepest reality. The word of Scripture is always about the fact that God loved us first (1 Jn 4:19). At creation it is God who speaks: "Fiat!" Only at the new creation does the response of man and creation come; the only true, possible response, as an echo: "Fiat!" God gave himself at creation: "Let it be done!" Only millions of years later—but what is that for God? "For a thousand years in your sight are but as yesterday when it is past" (Ps 90:4)—did it actually happen; when a small human being repeated: "Let it be done!" on behalf of all creation. Only then we "beheld his glory" (Jn 1:14).

Mary's Annunciation is still more the mystery of God's availability than of Mary's. Mary's "fiat" is the echo of God's "fiat". But the echo is truly not something secondary or nonessential. It follows, then, that what we call "the new creation" is in reality the completion of creation. After having worked with creation for six days, God rests on the seventh day: heaven waits breathlessly for creation's acceptance. When this acceptance finally comes, embodied in Mary's Yes, the eighth day begins, the octave that builds on the keynote, the new creation that does not reject anything of creation but, instead, completes and crowns it.

God cannot become man in a heart that only gives itself halfway. Our life could be so much richer if we learned from Mary to be wholehearted. God speaks to us through his Word, through his Church, through circumstances, and, if we listen carefully, through many secret inspirations. But instead of saying: "Behold, I am the handmaid of the Lord", the reaction is often: "I will not serve" (Jer 2:20). Our revolt against God is a foolish and hopeless battle, for our arms are too small to fight God. We prefer our own plans to God's plans and are astonished that the results are poor and the fruits are few. Mary had no plans of her own. She was open to God's plans. Throughout all eternity we will rejoice in Mary's Yes, which prepared a place in the world for God to become man.

A Yes to Both God and Man

Saying Yes to God always means, at the same time, saying Yes to man. Mary said Yes to God, and that Yes made her both Mother of God and Mother of mankind. Whoever opens himself to God lets God's love flow into the world. A student once asked me this question: "Who should really be in the center: God or man?" But that is a false alternative. We do not need to set God against man. The one who stands at the center is Jesus Christ; he is the focal point of the world and history; he is the Alpha and the Omega, and he is *both* God *and* man. A person becomes a complete human being only if he allows himself to be created anew in Christ. This is God's version of man. And that is why those who say an unconditional Yes to God like Mary, thus allowing Christ to be born in their hearts, are at the same time servants of the Lord and servants of men.

The Angelus

It has always been known by Christians that the greatest moment in history was the moment of the Annunciation. At the moment Mary answered Yes, the Word became flesh. Through the centuries, people of faith have chosen to remember this decisive event by praying the Angelus (see appendix 1). The ringing of the bells at midday in certain churches is a remnant of this practice. The one who prays the Angelus reenacts the scene of the Annunciation with its three-part structure, which is a fundamental structure in man's relationship with God: God's invitation, man's response, and the fruit: God who becomes a concrete and tangible reality in man. In his Apostolic Exhortation *Marialis Cultus* (February 2, 1974), Pope Paul VI chooses only two among the many traditional practices that have arisen in history to honor Mary. The Angelus and the rosary. The Pope realizes that the Angelus has retained its full timeliness.[1] One can hardly imagine a more fruitful way of sanctifying the most important moments of the day—morning, noon, and evening—than by praying this simple prayer.

[1] No. 41.

3

Mary Visits Elizabeth

Saint Luke recounts that Mary set out on a journey to her cousin Elizabeth. It was a long journey. Mary lived in the northern province of the country, Elizabeth in the south near Jerusalem, where her husband served at fixed times in the Temple.

Why This Visit?

Why did Mary want to visit Elizabeth after the message from the angel? One might have expected her to withdraw from all human contact in order to be completely available and present to the great wonder she was carrying, after she heard that the Lord was now present within her as her child. Should she not have devoted all her attention and love to the Divine Life growing within her like all the great mystics in history? Was it not silence and withdrawal that was necessary now? Alas, we have perhaps an erroneous concept of mysticism. Saying Yes to God also means saying Yes to men. To receive a mission from God always means to grow deeper into the human community. One receives nothing merely for himself. Everything must be shared.

According to tradition, Mary's intention was to assist and help her much older cousin during those months that preceded the child's birth. Saint Luke's account tells us that Mary stayed three months with Elizabeth, that is, up until the birth of John the Baptist, because Elizabeth was in her sixth month when Mary received the message from the angel.

But there were also other reasons for Mary's journey. She wanted to go and see the sign that had been given to her. According to the angel's message, Elizabeth, despite her age and though she was thought to be barren, had conceived a child. Mary wanted to see this sign, not because she doubted it, but because it belongs to the nature of a sign that it should be verified. One does not believe in a sign, one sees a sign. Mary was not able to pass over the sign that God had given her. Respect for the sign demanded that she go in order to assure herself, with her own eyes, that the sign had occurred. But surely Mary's first and foremost intention with this tiresome journey was to tell Elizabeth about the great thing that had happened in her. She felt an affinity with Elizabeth. Both of them had been blessed by God; a miracle had occurred in both of them, and the miracle in Elizabeth confirmed the miracle in Mary. Mary felt that Elizabeth must be the first to whom she proclaimed the good news. Every other woman would only shrug her shoulders. Elizabeth could receive Mary's message because God had visited her.

A Living Monstrance

Mary went "with haste", writes Saint Luke. She felt driven by a holy joy. Later, Saint Luke will mention the detail that the seventy disciples who are sent out by Jesus were not to greet anyone on the way (10:4).

The disciples may not waste time with drawn-out conversations and conventional phrases of courtesy. They must hurry; the Gospel must be spread. Mary was the first apostle, the first to proclaim the Good News. She thought of nothing else; she did not lose a single moment. Who does not remember Isaiah's words here: "How beautiful upon the mountains are the feet of him who brings glad tidings, who publishes peace, who brings good tidings of good, who publishes salvation, who says to Zion, 'Your God reigns'" (52:7)?

Mary carried Jesus. She was a ciborium and eventually became a monstrance. It soon began to be noticeable that she was with child. Mary carried her Creator. She bore the One who is greater than herself. Do we not all do the same? We bear one who is greater than ourselves, one who gives us our identity and worth. But we can forget that we bear him, as a priest who routinely carries Communion to the sick.

And Jesus let himself be carried. It was not he who decided. Already here he began to learn what he would do his whole life: let himself be carried by the Spirit. He never did his own will. "I do nothing on my own authority but speak thus as the Father taught me" (Jn

8:28, 29). He followed Mary wherever she went; he was completely dependent on her, as he is completely dependent on the priest in the Eucharist. But since Mary was overshadowed by the Spirit and was led by him in everything, the obedience of Jesus to Mary corresponded to his obedience to the Spirit. There was not a shadow of conflict. But is he not sometimes harshly treated and even completely dismayed when it is we who carry him?

Jesus Meets John

When after three or four days Mary came to the town where Elizabeth lived, she went into her house and greeted her. The greeting brought about a wonderful effect in Elizabeth: John the Baptist leaped in her womb. The forerunner recognized him for whom he would prepare the way. He was filled with a messianic joy: "But for you who fear my name the sun of righteousness shall rise, with healing in its wings. You shall go forth leaping like calves from the stall" (Mal 4:2). Mary had been a mother for only a few days, and already she was so filled with the Lord that he revealed himself through her transparent being. Jesus was not yet visible, but the one who came in contact with Mary was already influenced by him.

In reality, this is not primarily Mary's visit to Elizabeth but, rather, Christ's visit to John. But it was Mary who mediated the contact. She began even here what was to be her most important mission: to be a media-

trix of grace. Many are afraid that she could stand as a
barrier between God and man, but it is precisely her
task to facilitate contact. Wherever she comes with her
child, the grace of the child flows through her into the
world.

Mary did not say or tell anything; she brought her
message without words. She did not need to speak, she
"was", and what she was spoke for her. "The Visitation is one of your sweetest feasts, O Mother", writes
Brother Charles (1858–1916), "it is still more a feast
of the Lord's, for it is he who acts in and through you.
You proclaim the Good News, you preach the Gospel,
and you sanctify, not by your words, but by bearing
Jesus in silence to Elizabeth and John."

Elizabeth did not understand Mary's silent language
directly. It was through her child's mediation that she received insight into the great honor that was happening
in her: "How is it possible that the Mother of my Lord
should come to me?" "Filled with the Holy Spirit",
she spoke a prophetic word. Prophets often proclaim
a message whose reach goes far beyond their capacity
to understand. Elizabeth called Mary the "Mother of
the Lord". She was probably unclear about the Messiah's divine identity, but nonetheless she gave him the
title "Kyrios", a name that she immediately used afterward to indicate Yahweh: "That which the Lord
has promised to her shall be fulfilled." Without understanding the full meaning of her words, Elizabeth,
under the inspiration of the Holy Spirit, anticipated
the proclamation of the Council of Ephesus, which

solemnly declared in A.D. 431 that Mary was "Theotokos, the Mother of God".

The contact between these two women happened via the children. In this it can already be seen that the Lord came for the little ones and that the children are first in his kingdom. The first one to recognize him was a little unborn child. These two women were influenced by their children; it was the treasure they bore in the depths of themselves that gave their meeting an unimagined depth. What makes two people really encounter each other is not their thoughts or words, still less their expectations, but rather the fact that something that lies very deep within one meets something very deep in the other. "Abyssus abyssum invocat" (deep calls to deep) (Ps 42:7). No one knows beforehand if and when this will occur. But when it does, it is always because the Spirit comes over one or the other. Thanks to him, the horizontal relationship is crossed with the vertical line, and a cross is raised up. And only the Cross saves and sets free.

*Mary and Elizabeth Awaken
the Spirit in Each Other*

The Visitation is really a "Sacrament of Friendship". Mary shared the Holy Spirit she had received. But Elizabeth in her turn awakened the Spirit in Mary. Mary, who was silent up to this point, now sang her hymn of praise. She had to wait until a fellow human being, a friend, made the hidden spring pour forth. Despite the fact that she was the Mother of the Lord from the beginning, it was necessary that another person address her with this new name for it to be wholly true and real for her.

She burst out in jubilation. She did not, out of false humility, hide the "great things" that had been done in her. She knew it was the Lord who had done them and that only "his name is holy." She saw herself as a fruit of his mercy. She felt no need to efface herself in order to make God greater. Quite the contrary. It was in her high calling that God's greatness was seen. She dared to say the unprecedented words: "Henceforth all generations will call me blessed."

Why is it that a large part of Christianity is so afraid to praise Mary when she herself foretold in the Holy Spirit that the whole world would exalt her? Since her mission is identical to that of her Son's, it concerns the whole world and, therefore, must also be acknowledged by the whole world.

4

Mary and Joseph

While Saint Luke places greater emphasis on Mary's role in salvation history, Saint Matthew underlines Joseph's role. With Saint Luke, Joseph is completely in the background, while for Saint Matthew, however, it is he who leads the Holy Family. It is to him and not to Mary that the angel appears and says that he must flee to Egypt with Mary and Jesus (2:13). When the danger is over, because Herod is dead, it is again to him that the angel points out that they must return to Israel (2:19–20). And when they have come to Israel, it is yet again Joseph who receives in a dream the revelation that he must settle down in Galilee (2:22). When Saint Luke tells of Mary's Annunciation, he mentions nothing about Joseph's reaction. Saint Matthew, on the other hand, who does not say a word about the Annunciation, speaks exclusively about Joseph's attitude. We understand better why Saint Matthew speaks so readily about Joseph when we know he is writing for Jewish converts. He wants to show that all the Old Testament prophecies are fulfilled in Jesus. The Messiah would be David's son. He *is* David's son—says Saint Matthew, for Joseph is of David's line. It is thanks to Joseph that this fundamental prophecy about Jesus was fulfilled.

"Mary Was Engaged to Joseph"

Though engagement in Israel had binding power, and the betrothed were considered definitively bound to each other, marital life began only after the wedding. The marriage of Joseph and Mary had not yet taken place, and though Mary was already considered to be Joseph's wife, she still lived with her parents and Joseph lived with his parents.

When Mary entered into marriage with Joseph, it was not primarily to seek love and security from him. When she married, it was in order to obey God. She belonged to a people for whom marriage was practically a duty. To remain unmarried was a shame and a curse. Besides, it was not those entering into the marriage contract themselves who decided when and whom they would marry. It lay entirely in the hands of the parents. It was Joseph's father who sought out a girl who was suitable for his son, and his choice fell to Mary. When Mary's father agreed to this choice, Mary accepted it as God's will. God's will was the only thing that had any meaning for her. We may not forget that Mary was immaculate, free from original sin. That means that Mary did not react as we would. There was no egoism in her, not even a shadow of self-love. She did not reflect about herself; she did not desire to have anything for herself; she never said, "I like—I don't like." The only thing Mary liked was God's will, but it did not need to be constantly repeated; it was her being. Saint Luke, and all of tradition, has portrayed Mary as enveloped in deep silence. When one no longer speaks about one's likes or dislikes, a large amount of ordinary conversation disappears of itself. Mary was a big question mark before God. She was always on the alert: "What would you have me do now?" And then she did it. "And what do you will now? And now? . . ." Nothing was fixed with her. We plan far ahead and ask God to bless these plans. If he does not do this, we become annoyed or at least disappointed. Mary could never be disappointed with God, because she left everything open.

Joseph's Reaction

When Joseph discovered that Mary was with child, he could do nothing but doubt. Joseph knew nothing about the Annunciation, of course, and the great mystery that had happened to Mary. There are those who maintain that Mary must have spoken with Joseph about it and that Joseph's doubt had its origin in a holy fear: he would have felt unworthy to live with such a highly favored woman, who had conceived by the Holy Spirit. But it is clear from the angel's words that Joseph was unaware of the child's origins. "Joseph," says the angel, "do not fear to take Mary your wife, *for* [in Greek, *gar*] that which is conceived in her is of the Holy Spirit" (Mt 1:20). It was this that Joseph did not know, and, because he did not know it, he was afraid.

So perhaps we wonder: Why did Mary not speak with Joseph? It was something that concerned him to the highest degree and that would play a radical part in his life. There is a simple answer. How could Mary have spoken with Joseph? She was never alone with him. They did not yet live together, and to have a conversation before the wedding with one's betrothed without a witness was hardly conceivable in Israel.

When Joseph heard from the angel that the child in Mary's womb was a fruit of the Holy Spirit, it was undoubtedly an endless joy for him. He could again believe in Mary's purity, which perhaps in his deepest heart he had never ceased to do. He was to be a member of the family in which the Messiah would be born and raised. But at the same time, Joseph was forced to change his plans and rethink his life. Mary did not need to revise her dreams of the future when the angel came to her. No plans needed to be changed, since there were no plans. Joseph, on the other hand, was not a pure question mark before God as Mary was. To a certain extent, he was also an exclamation mark. He had his dreams and wishes. He had concrete ideas about marriage. It would not be as he had imagined. When now he must step aside for the Holy Spirit, it entailed a renunciation and possibly a difficult renunciation, but there was nothing in it that was bitter. He knew that this renunciation was a consequence of Mary's Yes to God. Together with Mary he pronounced his own Yes.[1]

We can imagine how from that day Joseph turned his eyes toward Mary with boundless respect. She was now the temple of the Holy Spirit, chosen by God before all other women on the earth to be the Mother of the Messiah.

The Virgin Birth a Myth?

Despite the fact that the Virgin Birth is clearly and unambiguously spoken of in the Gospels (Mt 1:16, 18–25; Lk 1:34–36; and perhaps also Jn 1:13, which according to some manuscripts must be read in the singular: "*he* is born, not of blood nor of the will of the flesh nor of the will of man, but of God" and in that case alludes both to the Word's eternal birth within the Trinity and his birth in time of a Virgin), certain exegetes and theologians question the historical reality of the event. The miracle seems to be too great to be true. But then one can ask oneself if the miracle of the Incarnation is not much greater. In reality one notices that those theologians who have difficulty believing in the Virgin Birth often have the tendency to interpret the Incarnation in a way that undermines its very substance. In a reply to Hans Küng, Walter Kasper

[1] Cf. Adrienne von Speyr, *Handmaid of the Lord* (San Francisco: Ignatius Press, 1985), 63.

formulated with great precision the decisive question:
"Who is Jesus Christ? Is he a human person in whom
God revealed himself through speech and action, or
is he God's co-eternal Son who has become man in
history?"[2] If Jesus is God, we need not be astonished
that he is born not "by man's willing it".

That Joseph was not the father of Jesus can be seen in
many texts, even in the Synoptic Gospels, where Jesus
speaks of his relationship to the Father. Already as a
twelve-year-old, he corrected Mary when she mildly
reproached him because his "father" and she had been
looking for him in vain for three days: "How is it that
you sought me? Did you not know that I must be
in my Father's house?" (Lk 2:48–49). His father was
not Joseph, but the Father in heaven. In the Gospel
of Matthew, we hear Jesus say that he and the Father
are one: "All things have been delivered to me by my
Father; and no one knows the Son except the Father,
and no one knows the Father except the Son and any
one to whom the Son chooses to reveal him" (11:27).
In this context, Hans Urs von Balthasar writes:

> In view of texts like these, which stand for many
> others, let us go abruptly to the question: Could this
> man, who had such a unique relationship to the "Fa-
> ther in heaven", to whom he owed his existence, en-

[2] Quoted by Peter Hünermann, "Zur Auseinandersetzung zwis-
chen Hans Küng und dem kirchlichen Lehramt", *Geist und Leben*,
February 1980, 13.

trusted himself, and unreservedly gave himself back —could he owe his existence to another father at the same time? Could he, putting it crudely, have two fathers? Did he have to acknowledge two fathers as the source of his existence? . . . And could Jesus, who, after all, enjoined the observance of the Ten Commandments (Mk 10:19), have himself transgressed against one that was so vital to all ancient cultures? And supposing he owed his existence as much to the man Joseph as he did to his heavenly Father, and so had to keep the commandment, would not this double paternity have led to certain schizophrenia? The only way out of the dilemma would be to say that he owes his existence to his heavenly Father like any other man whose immortal soul comes from the Creator, who plants this soul in the new being at the moment of the parents' procreative act. If this were the case, Jesus would be, to be sure, a pious man who honors his parents and in doing so also thinks of his Creator, but would be in no respect better or worse than we are, and he would have been just as incapable as we are of saying "no one knows the Father but the Son."[3]

Theologically speaking, the Virgin Birth is also the prerequisite for Mary's unique place in the Church. Mary is not only called to be the Mother of God's Son, she will also eventually, according to God's plan,

[3] Hans Urs von Balthasar, "Conceived by the Holy Spirit, Born of the Virgin Mary", in Joseph Cardinal Ratzinger and Hans Urs von Balthasar, *Mary: The Church at the Source*, trans. Adrian Walker (Communio; San Francisco: Ignatius Press, 2005), 148–49.

become his Bride, as the image and embodiment of the Church. Her entire existence is totally directed to Christ. It is to him she will belong, to him she has been betrothed, to him she will be presented as a pure virgin (2 Cor 11:2). She represents the holy city, the new Jerusalem, adorned as a bride to meet her husband (Rev 21:2). Yes, she is the bride, the wife of the Lamb (Rev 21:9). Therefore she could not be Joseph's bride in the ordinary sense. There is an exclusiveness in her vocation that makes her belong both body and soul to Jesus and him alone. As the New Eve, she belongs to the New Adam. The new human couple that established the New Covenant and restored what the first human couple had destroyed is not Joseph and Mary, but Jesus and Mary. She is the model of the Virginal Church and of every person who is called to belong to Christ with an exclusive and total love.

Ever Virgin

It has always been the Church's conviction, a conviction that was also shared by the Reformers, that Mary remained a virgin after Jesus' birth and, thus, had no other children than Jesus. In a sermon on Candlemas day 1546, Luther said: "A virgin before the conception and birth, she has remained a virgin also at the birth and after it."[4] Calvin condemned those who claimed that Mary had other children besides Jesus.

[4] As quoted by Max Thurian, *Mary, Mother of the Lord*, trans. Neville B. Cryer (London: Faith Press, 1963), 39.

If one looks only at the New Testament texts, one cannot with absolute certainty draw any conclusions about Mary's perpetual virginity. But by what has been said about Mary's vocation to be the archetype of the Church "without stain or wrinkle", it follows that a temporary virginity would be meaningless. If one has, besides this, understood that virginity is not so much a question of abstinence as to be "anxious about the affairs of the Lord, how to be holy in body and spirit" (1 Cor 7:34), it is clear that virginity cannot be only "for a time". God does not take back his gifts; he completes what he has begun. How could Mary give birth to other children after giving birth to him who "is before all things" (Col 1:17)? How could anything be added to him who is the New Adam, the origin of the new human race? The fact that the New Testament speaks of the brothers and sisters of Jesus is no obstacle to Mary's virginity. Everyone knows that Hebrew uses the same word for both brother and cousins. The term "brother" can even mean any relative whatsoever. It is true that in Greek there are different words to indicate different forms of kinship, but we must not forget that the Greek of the Gospels bears traces of Aramaic throughout the entire text.

Why would Jesus have said to his Mother on the Cross: "Woman, behold, your son!" (Jn 19:26), referring her to John, who would take his place, if Mary had had other children who could take care of her?

The fact that Saint Luke writes of Mary that "she gave birth to her first-born son" (2:7) has nothing to do with other children in the future. The first son was usually called the first-born, regardless of whether or not there were more children.

5

Mother of God

During the time between the Annunciation and the birth of Christ, Mary was filled with a quiet joy and an interior longing. She had already received Jesus, but she longed for him to grow and show himself at last. She longed to see him "face to face" whom she already carried within herself. "Let me see your face, let me hear your voice" (Song 2:14).

Mary's Advent

Is there not a great similarity between Mary's situation and our own? During the time she was expecting her child, she was a unique example for every Christian. What we are waiting for is already within us. We already *have* that for which we are waiting. Yes, we have already received what is essential. We are blessed. The Lord is with us. He lives in us by the Holy Spirit. His life has been grafted into ours through baptism. But we long to see him. We rejoice and give thanks for what we have received, but at the same time we long for what we have received to come forth into the full light of day. Mary, and every Christian worth the name, is filled with both fervent longing and grateful joy, because the one who has come continues to come.

In her expectation, Mary summed up the entire world's longing for a savior. She was familiar with the Scriptures, whose message no one had ever understood like she had. The Holy Spirit who overshadowed her is the same one who inspired those holy words. She knew that the whole Old Covenant was one long, drawn-out period of advent and that this immeasurable, universal longing was now concentrated in her. She could do nothing but tremble when she thought that the moment had now arrived for the longing of mankind to be fulfilled.

A mother who is expecting her child often dreams about what the child will look like. She looks at her husband and imagines that the child will perhaps look like him. For Mary, it did not help to look at Joseph to know anything about the child. She had been touched by the Holy Spirit, and him she had never seen. She could not create a concrete image of her child. Thus her expectation was completely open: because it had no clear contours, the possibilities were endless. She merely let God do his work in her.

Theotokos

The child to whom Mary gave birth in Bethlehem was not a small human being in whom God had come to dwell in a special way. No, this human child was God. And Mary who had given birth to this child was the

Mother of God. "To the wonderment of nature you bore your Creator, yet remained a Virgin after as before" (*Alma Redemptoris Mater*). Is this not unbelievable? Is it not a beautiful story, too beautiful to be true? Should it not be considered mythology? On the contrary, it is a sober and factual assertion: Since Jesus is God, Mary who gave birth to Jesus is the Mother of God. As early as the year 431, long before the Church was divided, the Council Fathers in Ephesus laid down that the title Theotokos (the Mother of God) must be ascribed to Mary.[1]

Mary was nevertheless the origin only of Jesus' human nature, not of his divine nature. How could she then be called God's Mother? The answer is that one is mother, not of a nature, but of a person. Despite the fact that Jesus has two natures, he is only *one* Person, the second Person of the Holy Trinity. Is it not always so that the child a mother brings into the world is much more than what she and her husband can bring about? For every mother, the child is not the fruit of her own effort but, rather, God's gift. What a mother can give birth to by her own power is a living body. The fact that this new creature is a person is due, not to her own merit, but to God's. But for all that, there is no one who would fail to recognize that she is the mother of this child. So Mary is also the Mother of

---

[1] Heinrich Denzinger, *Compendium of Creeds, Definitions, and Declarations on Matters of Faith and Morals*, ed. Peter Hünermann, Eng. trans. ed. Robert Fastiggi and Anne Englund Nash, 43rd ed. (San Francisco: Ignatius Press, 2012), no. 251, p. 94.

God, because she is the Mother of Jesus as a divine Person, despite the fact that she gave birth to him only *sarkikōs* (according to the flesh).[2]

By calling Mary "Theotokos", the Council of Ephesus at the same time affirmed that Jesus Christ is true God. It is not possible to separate Mariology from Christology. The one who refuses Mary the title of "Mother of God" unavoidably, possibly unconsciously or involuntarily, brushes up against the ancient heresy that regarded the distinction between the two natures of Christ to be a distinction between a divine person and a human person. The Nestorians could not imagine a human nature to be anything other than a human person. They believed Christ could be fully human only if he were a human person.

It is easy to see that this is not mere theological speculation but, rather, entails the serious weighing of consequences with respect to faith in the Incarnation itself. Instead of confessing with Scripture that "the Word was made Flesh", Nestorianism teaches (at least as it has been understood by tradition) that God united himself with a human being who was already existing beforehand. God would thus not have been born as a man but, instead, would have united himself with a human being, so that there would indeed be an intimate relationship between God's Word and the man Christ, but without the Word being true man and without the

[2] Ibid.

man being called God. In his second letter to Nestorius, Saint Cyril of Alexandria writes: "For this was not an ordinary man who was at first begotten of the holy Virgin, and then the Word descended upon him: rather, [the Word] united flesh to himself from his mother's womb and is said to have undergone begetting in the flesh in order to take to himself flesh of his own. . . . For this reason [the holy Fathers] have not hesitated to speak of the holy Virgin as the Mother of God."[3] The Council Fathers in Ephesus officially supported this text from the letter of Bishop Cyril.

Luther never questioned the teaching of the Council of Ephesus. He wrote:

> This council (of Ephesus) did not establish anything new in the faith, but defended the ancient faith against the new vagueness of Nestorius. Indeed the article according to which Mary is Mother of God has been in the Church from the beginning and has not been newly produced by the council but on the contrary [is] contained in the gospel or in holy Scripture. For in St. Luke (1:32) we find that the angel Gabriel announces to the Virgin that she must bear the Son of the Most High and Elizabeth says: "whence comes it that the Mother of the Lord should come to me?" And the angels at Christmas together sing: "unto us is born this day a Saviour which is Christ the Lord." In the same way St. Paul (Gal. 4:4): "God has sent his Son, born of a woman." These words which I hold

[3] Ibid.

to be true surely support quite strongly that Mary is the Mother of God.[4]

The Mother of God for the Sake of the World

When a child leaves his mother's womb, he takes his first steps out into the world. To give birth to a child is at the same time to be separated from him. This first separation is only the beginning of ever deeper and more painful partings and quests by which the child gains his independence and discovers his own calling. For every mother, it is a difficult and often painful process to accept these successive departures and allow her child to free himself more and more from her in order to go his own way. In Mary's case, this task was unbelievably radical and demanding. On the one hand, she was truly Mother in the full sense of the word. Jesus was her child. She could say to him: "You are my bone and my flesh!" (Gen 29:14). She loved Jesus as every mother loves her child, or, one should say, much more, since her freedom from sin made her capacity to love much greater. But, on the other hand, she knew that the child's father was not Joseph but God and that God had destined this child to save the world from its sin. She knew that she could not lay any claims on her child, that she had given birth to him for the world. Bethlehem means "house of bread".

---

[4] As quoted by Max Thurian, *Mary, Mother of the Lord*, trans. Neville B. Cryer (London: Faith Press, 1963), 76.

Her child is the "living bread which came down from heaven" (Jn 6:51). Mary had to learn from the beginning to share this bread: with the shepherds, with the wise men, with all who came to see. For her it was not a question of pressing her child to her heart. She had to allow him to be available to all.

Mary had already begun to experience something of the call to universality that her Yes entailed for her at the Annunciation, a call that reached its zenith when she became the cosmic woman spoken of in the Book of Revelation (12:1). To give birth to Jesus is to administer the Eucharist. There can be no borders here: he must be distributed "from the rising of the sun to its setting" (Mal 1:11). Perhaps only a mother can understand what it means in the way of pain and self-denial to have to "distribute" her child from beginning to end.

As a mother, Mary had the mission of raising her Son. She had to teach him to be ready to give his life. She had authority over this child who was by far greater than she herself was. To accept and exercise this authority was for her a source of humility. Nothing makes a person so small as to receive a mission that far and away surpasses her capacities. Every spiritual director who is called to guide someone who is much closer to God than he is will gladly confirm this. In our time, there are many who flee from this task as leader and hide behind beautiful words about equality and shared responsibility. Mary did not do this. Together with Joseph, she guided and raised her child, for that was God's will. And Jesus listened to Mary. "Blush, O dust and ashes, and be ashamed to be proud", says Saint Bernard of Clairvaux (1090–1153); "God humbles Himself, and do you exalt your self? God submits to man, and do you desire to domineer over your fellow-man?"[5]

---

[5] *Sermons of Saint Bernard on Advent and Christmas, including the Famous Treatise on the Incarnation Called "Missus Est"*, trans. J. C. Hedley, O.S.B. (London: Washbourne; New York: Benziger, 1909), 31.

6

Jesus Is Presented in the Temple

"And when the time came for their purification according to the law of Moses, they brought him up to Jerusalem to present him to the Lord" (Lk 2:22).

"For Their Sake I Consecrate Myself" *(John 17:19)*

Since according to the law the first-born son belonged to God, the parents could not consider him their child before they had redeemed him from God.

> "Every first-born of man among your sons you shall redeem. And when in time to come your son asks you, 'What does this mean?' you shall say to him, 'By strength of hand the LORD brought us out of Egypt, from the house of bondage. For when Pharaoh stubbornly refused to let us go, the LORD slew all the first-born of man and the first-born of cattle. Therefore I sacrifice to the LORD all the males that first open the womb; but all the first-born of my sons I redeem.' It shall be as a mark on your hand or frontlets between your eyes; for by a strong hand the LORD brought us out of Egypt." (Ex 13:13–16)

Mary and Joseph subjected themselves to this pre-
scribed ritual. Though Jesus was above the law, "The
Son of man is lord of the sabbath" (Lk 6:5), he was
"born under the law, to redeem those who were under
the law" (Gal 4:4-5).

Saint Luke does not say, however, that Mary and
Joseph "redeemed" Jesus but, rather, that they presented him to the Lord. In this way he brings out the
deep meaning of the law's precept, that the first-born
son shall be publicly recognized as belonging to the
Lord. Truly Jesus would not be redeemed from God!
If anyone belonged to God from all eternity it was
he. His entire life had only one meaning: to return to
the Father from whom he had come forth. "I came
from the Father" (Jn 16:28). Mary went to the Temple to consecrate her Son to God. Though she was his
Mother, he did not belong to her, but to the Father.
The Father would have complete freedom to use him
and lead him where he willed.

Who does not see that Mary is an image of the
Church? The time would come when the Church
would present the Body and Blood of Christ each day
as a pleasing sacrifice to the Father. Mary began to do
what she would later do unceasingly as *Mater ecclesia*
until the end of time. She was able to say to God what
the Church so often repeats during the Mass: that she
offered of his "own gifts" (the first Eucharistic Prayer).
God places the Body and Blood of Christ in the hands
of the Church so that she will have something precious
to offer, something worthy of him. In the same way,

Mary received her Son, who was also God's Son, so that she could present the most precious sacrifice that had ever been offered to God. God was already in the process of creating a Church for himself. In Mary, the contours of the Church were gradually beginning to come into focus.

The old Simeon who took the child in his arms was an image of the heavenly Father who received Mary's offering. She received a visible sign that her offering was pleasing to God.

The Dialogue between Mary and Simeon

The dialogue between Mary and Simeon is at the center of Luke's account of the Presentation of Jesus in the Temple. Even though Mary did not say a word, we can nevertheless speak of a dialogue. Simeon spoke, and Mary answered with her quiet listening. Simeon did not speak in a vacuum. He spoke directly into Mary's openness. Mary's way of having a dialogue was to be silent, to listen, to keep and ponder everything in her heart. Everyone who seeks contact with Mary, who looks to her and seeks to live with her, receives something of her silence and openness. Is it not so that the typical Marian prayers, the Litany of Loreto and the rosary, are prayers that bring peace? The monotonous repetition makes a person calm and still. By these prayers Mary leads us into her own contemplation.

Truly Simeon and Mary were created to understand

each other. Both were filled with the Holy Spirit. They could carry on a dialogue at a deep level. We know that Mary was filled with the Holy Spirit. She had been overshadowed by the Spirit at the Annunciation, and for nine months she carried God under her heart. But Simeon, too, even though he belonged to the Old Covenant, was filled with the Spirit. Saint Luke, who shows great love for the Spirit, speaks three times of Simeon's relationship to the Spirit: "The Holy Spirit was upon him" (2:25), "it had been revealed to him by the Holy Spirit that he should not see death before he had seen the Lord's Christ" (2:26), and "inspired by the Spirit he came into the temple" (27).

Simeon came from the Old Covenant, but at the moment he met Mary and took Jesus in his arms, he became a Christian. The prophetic charism he exercised in the Old Covenant now received a new object. He gazed into the future of Jesus and Mary and became Christianity's first prophet and theologian. He saw that, for many, it would be difficult to recognize God in a child, in a human being, in a suffering human being. It would be easier to believe in a God who lived in a distant heaven than to believe in a God who identified himself with man. There is an abyss between believing in God and believing in Jesus Christ. One must go over the threshold. God was compelled to use hard means on the way to Damascus to bring Saint Paul over the threshold. To believe in Jesus Christ makes us look, to the eyes of unbelievers, like children who believe in fairly tales. Jesus was destined to be the fall and the rising of many. Some fall over him, and others are saved by him.

Simeon also saw how Jesus and Mary shared the same mission. It constituted a unity. One cannot separate Jesus from Mary or Mary from Jesus. Sometimes it is Jesus who leads us to Mary. It was this way for Saint John. When he stood at the foot of the Cross, he was directed by Jesus to Mary: "Behold, your mother!" (Jn 19:27). Sometimes it is Mary who leads us to Jesus. This is how it was for Saint Joseph. He would never have come so close to Jesus if he had not discovered Mary among the girls in Nazareth. The old Simeon saw prophetically how the call of Jesus was also the call of Mary. Every blow of the hammer that drove the nails into Jesus' hands and feet found an echo in Mary's heart. Nothing was done to Jesus that did not also wound Mary.

"A sword will pierce through your own soul" (Lk 2:35). To be Mother of the Messiah was not only to be Mother of a king, but also to be Mother of a man of sorrows. Mary was surely familiar with the passage of Isaiah about the Lord's Suffering Servant. The prophecy of Simeon made real for her what she often heard: "He was despised and rejected by men; a man of sorrows, and acquainted with grief; and as one from whom men hide their faces he was despised, and we esteemed him not" (Is 53:3). Every suffering that befell Jesus also befell Mary. The sword that pierced her was the Cross that would be planted in the center of her heart. The sword would inflict a gaping wound, but it would never be visible. Mary would not receive the stigmata like Saint Francis of Assisi. She remained true to herself. This wound she also hid in her heart. Mary was not called to show or reveal anything. Though she shared in the redemptive work of Jesus, she did not share in his preaching. What Mary did was to give an echo; she was the fertile soil in which the seed bore fruit a hundredfold.

We see how Mary, pierced by a sword, is an image of the Church even here. It will be the mission of the Church to fill up in her body what is lacking in the sufferings of Christ (Col 1:24). All the children of the Church must go the way of the Cross in one way or another, for the disciple is not greater than the Master (Mt 10:24). Mary was the first to go this way with him. She set in motion a new movement, a movement of com-passion, in the original meaning of the word. Everyone must take part, in both death and resurrection. Before Mary was taken up body and soul into heaven, she had to be the Mother of sorrows. Her life was a living prophecy. The Church needs only to look at her in order to have a clear idea of herself, of her present and future.

The dialogue between Simeon and Mary can teach us how to carry on a dialogue at a deep level. Simeon spoke, but only because he was inspired by the Holy Spirit. He had something to say, because what he said came from the Holy Spirit. Mary listened. She was pure openness that allowed her to be filled by the words. She did not discuss. She did not comment. She received and nothing more. Simeon spoke, though he knew he was the least and that Mary was much greater. He spoke, because he had received a mission to speak. Mary listened, and it was natural for her to listen. She did not reflect about herself. She did not think: It is really I who should be speaking, since I have received the most from the Holy Spirit. Simeon and Mary both did exactly what they were supposed to do. And that is why their conversation resounds through history, even to this day.

7

Jesus Is Lost in the Temple

When Jesus was twelve years old, he was allowed to take part in the pilgrimage to Jerusalem (Lk 2:41–50). Something happened to him in the Temple that also had great consequences for Mary. Up to this point, Jesus had apparently been a rather "normal" boy. Mary raised him as a mother usually raises her child. She was able to follow his development step by step. She had a certain overview of what happened with him. She took the initiative, and Jesus responded. There is no reason to give credence to the stories in the apocryphal Gospels where Jesus would have worked miracles even as a child. No, as a child he behaved like all the other children in Nazareth. He was like them in all things but sin (cf. Heb 4:15). It is true, he was not stubborn or aggressive, lazy or envious, but his behavior was not especially sensational in any way, since no one in Nazareth seemed to have guessed he was sent by God as the Savior of the world. He learned to read and write like all other boys. Like all other children, he constantly asked Mary and Joseph questions, not because he was playing the role of a child, but because he was inquisitive, and there were many things he did not

know. Together with Mary and Joseph he sang psalms
and listened to the prophecies of Isaiah. He stood at
the carpenter bench with Joseph and learned the se-
crets of carpentry. All of this was completely natural
and obvious.

The Identity of Jesus

Something happened in the Temple, however, that
shattered this obviousness and let a hidden dimension
in him come into daylight. It seems as though there
in the Temple, Jesus became aware of his identity in a
new way. One can imagine that the Temple made an
overwhelming impression on him, that his consciousness as Son was suddenly awakened and made him
forget everything: Mary, Joseph, and the whole company of travelers. He was not as ordinary as he looked.
He lived in a unique relationship with the Father. For
Mary, this meant she experienced, for the first time
concretely, that there was another force in his life to
which he had to yield. She could no longer foresee or
direct his development. It was not only with Joseph
she had to share her task as parent, but also with him
who is his true Father: God. The prophecy foretold by
the old Simeon, that her soul would be pierced with
a sword, was already beginning to be a reality. She
experienced painfully that her child did not belong to
her. At every moment a new mission could come from
heaven that she would have to give him the freedom
to carry out.

We are perhaps surprised that Mary and Joseph did not immediately look for Jesus in the Temple. They had, of course, presented him there as a newborn child and, by doing so, made the Temple his true home. Mary might have guessed she could find her child there. But Mary did not yet live in the fullness of revelation. On the contrary, it was her task to be God's instrument at the moment of revelation itself. She had to walk the way of faith just as we do, or, rather, even more than we do, for she did not have the same insight as we do about her Son's identity. She undoubtedly knew Jesus was chosen by God to save Israel, but could she imagine that he was one with God to such a degree that he would be said to be "light from light, true God from true God"?

"I Sought Him"

Furthermore, it was right for her to seek him. The fact that he was lost for three days undoubtedly alluded to his death and burial: even then she would call out to him for three days.

Like Mary, many of us have a sense of having lost Jesus, that he is absent. But the difference between Mary and us is that his absence caused her to suffer unbearable torments and to seek him with a fervent longing. Is it not Mary whom we hear in the Song of Songs when the bride complains: "I sought him but found him not; I called him, but he gave no answer. . . . I adjure you, O daughters of Jerusalem, if you find my beloved, that you tell him I am sick with love" (5:6, 8)?

That God allowed Mary—and allows us—to seek and long without answering us immediately can only bewilder the one who has not understood the meaning of the search and the longing. Desire is the very best preparation for receiving what we desire and receiving it in proper measure. Desire digs out new depths. Desire enlarges us so that we contain much more. When God wants to give us something great, he first increases our capacity. Otherwise, too much would be lost. He cannot pour ten liters of wine into an inkwell. The inkwell must first become a bucket. This happens by way of desire. It is thus a sign, not of less love, but of greater love that God allows us at times to wait and search. He wants to give us more than we can receive right now. But we usually misunderstand him. Instead of preparing ourselves and making our interior larger by desiring, we believe he has forgotten us, and we give up. By seeking until she found, Mary was able to anticipate something of the Resurrection joy that would be hers when she met her Risen Son for the first time.

"Why?"

When Mary asked Jesus: "Son, why have you treated us so? Behold, your father and I have been looking for you anxiously", Jesus answered: "How is it that you sought me? Did you not know I must be in my Father's house?" Jesus corrected Mary's manner of speaking: Why do you say *my father* has sought me? I was in *my Father's house*, of course. There, in his Father's house, Jesus experienced more clearly than ever that the name "father" was not suitable for Joseph. In truth, he could call only God Father. Jesus showed Mary that he was conscious of his exclusive Son-relationship with the Father. God is his Father to such a high degree that he cannot have any human father. During his public life, Jesus often called God his Father and thus caused offense to the Jews. Saint John writes that the Jews wanted to kill Jesus because he called God his Father and, by doing so, claimed to be equal to God (5:18).

"But they did not understand what he said to them." Not even Mary understood Jesus' words. It was now time for her to enter into the darkness, which sooner or later comes to every person who is seriously seeking God. "When one is abiding under the shadow of the Almighty there will be no light, but that is only because God's Presence is so near", writes Corrie Ten Boom.[1] Jesus had lifted an edge of the veil that hid his divine identity, and instead of light it became dark. Mary was forced to enter a new school, where it became more difficult for her to understand. She experienced an ever thicker darkness, which reached its peak when she witnessed her Son's utmost humiliation at the foot of the Cross. Mary's "*Why* have you treated us so?" was her

[1] Corrie Ten Boom, *Tramp for the Lord* (New York: Jove Books, 1978), 59.

own version of the Son's dramatic "My God, my God, why have you abandoned me?" How could Mary understand, when not even Jesus could understand his Father? "If you understand," says Saint Augustine, "it is not God."

Here in Jerusalem, Jesus showed that he was not only the child of his Mother but that he belonged first of all to his Father and had to go the way the Father would show him. Mary never prevented her child from going the way of the Father. She always gave Jesus the freedom he needed to carry out his mission. But now, for the first time, it appeared that his mission was driving him away from her. The call of Mary, and of every Christian, consists in giving Jesus free reign, so that he can do his will without any hindrance.

The Holy Family

The scenes in Jerusalem are a warning and hint of the way of the Cross that Mary must go. But only a first hint, because Jesus returned with Mary and Joseph to Nazareth, where he was "obedient to them". For two thousand years, the Holy Family has been the ideal for every human family. Jesus, Mary, and Joseph reflect the Divine Family of the Holy Trinity, where together the Father, Son, and Holy Spirit form an ineffable community of Love.

Like every family, the Holy Family also knew joy and suffering, but in greater proportions: joy and suffering were deeper. Deep suffering because Mary and

Joseph could not follow Jesus into the incomprehensible mystery in which he lived and of which he could not speak before his hour had come. And deep joy, because they completely forgot themselves and lived only for their child. They realized in a perfect way what Saint-Exupéry wrote about the ideal friendship: that it consists, not in two people sitting opposite each other gazing at each other, but, rather, in two people sitting next to each other looking together at a third person, Jesus. In the same way Mary and Joseph looked at Jesus.

8

Mary at Cana

"On the third day there was a marriage at Cana in Galilee" (Jn 2:1). These words "on the third day" are important. They remind us of what we say in the Creed: "[He] rose again on the third day in accordance with the Scriptures." For Saint John, the wedding at Cana has something to do with the Paschal mystery. Jesus gave his life for his Church on the Cross. He entered into an indissoluble marriage with his bride, a marriage that was definitively sealed on Easter Sunday. At Cana the eternal wedding feast was in a mysterious way already realized. Jesus later says the kingdom of heaven is like a wedding banquet (Mt 22:2). This wedding banquet is the object of our longing. But here again, we see the goal is already present from the beginning. We cannot strive for the goal if we have not seen it in a vision. In the story of the wedding feast at Cana, we *receive* that vision. We already have a glimpse of what awaits us.

"The Mother of Jesus Was There"

"The Mother of Jesus was there", writes Saint John. Of course! Just as Mary was present at the end when Jesus died on the Cross for his beloved Bride the Church, she was also present at the beginning. The Church is embodied in Mary. For the Church, it is enough to look at the ideal to know how she should be and act. Mary's way of acting at the wedding feast of Cana teaches us very much, not only about her, but also about the Church and about ourselves.

When the wine ran out, Mary said to Jesus: "They have no wine." Mary's eyes were opened to the needs of the newly married couple. She showed even here that she was not only the Mother of Jesus, but also the Mother of all people. It is typical of her to be especially attentive to the distress and concerns within the house of the Church. Where there is a need, Mary is there. But is Jesus not enough? Jesus would surely not have performed a miracle at Cana if Mary had not been there. It is true Mary is not on the same level as Jesus. We have only one Savior and Mediator, Jesus Christ. Mary stands between him and us, not in order to separate but to unite. She turns to Jesus so that he will look at us, and she turns to us so that we will look at Jesus.

Mary's Prayer

She turned first to Jesus: "They have no wine." She did not interfere herself. She presented the need of the couple and left it all to Jesus. In this way, she showed that only he could save us in our need. Mary gave us an extremely concrete lesson in prayer. Her simple words are for all times a model for Christian prayer. She did not tell Jesus what to do. She had no personal plans that she wished for him to carry out. She pointed out the need and nothing more. There is another Mary in the Gospel who acted in exactly the same way. When Lazarus her brother was sick, she sent a message to Jesus: "Lord, he whom you love is ill" (Jn 11:3). She did not say that Jesus must heal her brother. She left everything in his hands. And Jesus did not heal Lazarus. He waited until Lazarus was dead in order to show that he was not only a faith healer but the resurrection and the life.

Saint John of the Cross quotes these two places in the Gospel of John when he explains how a person should pray for himself and others. In a little commentary he writes: "The discreet lover does not care to ask for what she lacks and desires, but only indicates this need that the Beloved may do what He pleases. When the Blessed Virgin spoke to her beloved Son at the wedding feast in Cana in Galilee, she did not ask directly for the wine, but merely remarked: *They have no wine* [Jn. 2:3]."[1] Saint John of the Cross gives three reasons why it is best simply to point out one's need and pain, rather than tell God directly what he must do. First of all, God knows better than we do what we need. Secondly, the Beloved feels a deeper

[1] *Spiritual Canticle*, stanza 2, 8, in *The Collected Works of Saint John of the Cross*, trans. Kieran Kavanaugh, O.C.D., and Otilio Rodriguez, O.C.D. (Washington, D.C.: ICS Publications, Institute of Carmelite Studies, 1979), 427.

compassion when he sees an absolute surrender and trust in the suffering person. And thirdly, the danger of self-love is less: by trying to force God to give us certain gifts, we risk feeding our ego.[2]

This must not be understood to mean we should never pray for "things". We need to realize Saint John of the Cross is writing for people who are in the "state of proficients" and "in which the spiritual espousal is effected".[3] He indicates a direction. He shows a way. Some people are only capable of this method of praying for things. It would be totally wrong to refuse them such a prayer on the basis of Saint John of the Cross and thereby deprive them of the only prayer they can manage at that particular stage of their spiritual development.

But the fact remains, there is only one thing for which we may pray unconditionally, and that is God himself. When he gives himself, he gives all. The first part of the Our Father raises us to that level. There God stands at the center: hallowed be *Thy* name, *Thy* kingdom come, *Thy* will be done. It is true we ask for things for ourselves afterward, but these special prayers must always be rooted in a total surrender and an unreserved obedience. The nearer a person comes to God, the more he places the emphasis on the first part of the Our Father. And when he prays for himself or for others, he does it more and more like Mary:

[2] Ibid.
[3] Ibid., prologue, 3, p. 409.

she points out the need and then lets God help as he himself wills.

Not all the worry and concern we have for the world is from God. A concern that makes us anxious, tense, discouraged, and bitter shows we are not on God's wavelength. We try to carry the world on our own small shoulders, instead of placing it in God's hands. The one who places the world in God's love continues to suffer with those who are suffering, but his suffering is marked by a deep inner peace. For he knows God loves everyone and is able to transform everything that is evil into good. He knows God has the last word, and that word is a word of love.

"Woman"

"Woman," Jesus answered, "what have you to do with me?" It is very unusual that Jesus addressed his Mother as "woman", and it must have a special meaning. When a Jew turned to his mother, he said as a rule: "my mother". Saint John writes that Jesus also called Mary "woman" on the Cross, when he gave John to her as her son (19:26). Jesus wanted to make clear to Mary that the time had come for a new relationship between them. She was no longer the mother of her child, with all that that entailed of motherly love and care. Jesus had now begun to carry out the mission he received from his Father, and Mary had to give him the free-dom to go in the Father's ways. Even the expression "What have you to do with me?" clearly points out a distancing. But at the same time, the address "woman", which reminds us of "the woman" in Genesis 3:15 ("I will put enmity between you and the woman"), has a positive meaning. In the relationship that would exist from now on between Jesus and Mary, Jesus would be the New Adam, the beginning of the new mankind, and Mary, the New Eve, who would stand at his side as his helper and companion. Man, the first as well as the new (cf. Gen 1:27), is always man and woman: Adam-Eve, Jesus-Mary, Christ-Church. Jesus and Mary are now the new human couple who will restore what was destroyed by the first human couple. Mary and Jesus act no longer as Mother and Son, but as bride and bridegroom.

Jesus' Hour

Jesus added: "My hour has not yet come." We find the expression "my hour", "his hour", many times in the Gospel of John, and it always points to the decisive moment of revelation at Jesus' death and Resurrection. Jesus said: "My hour has not yet come" at Cana. In his great farewell discourse, he said: "Father, the hour has come; glorify your Son" (17:1). When Jesus pointed out that his hour had not yet come, he in no way meant that the moment for him to perform miracles had not come. On the contrary, it was part of his mission to show through many "signs" that the kingdom of heaven was now in the midst of the people. But for Jesus, it was too early to perform this particular miracle. If he brought forth wine through a miracle, he would in reality be acting as host and bridegroom, and the hour for this had not yet come. Only at his death and Resurrection could he act as bridegroom.

But despite the fact that his hour would come only when it was time for him to die and rise, it was nevertheless called forth for a brief moment by Mary's faith. The first miracle Jesus performed became, thanks to Mary's intervention, a definitive sign by which the final goal could be perceived: that God celebrates a wedding with mankind. How important Mary's initiative was stands out even more clearly when we remember that the miracle at Cana was the only sign in the life of Jesus where his hour was anticipated.

Mary's faith was so great that she had the ability to make God's hour come, even though it had not yet come. Mary appeared only once in this way, but it was enough to show that she, like a new Esther, is a queen who has power over the King.

Mother of Good Counsel

Mary turned to Jesus to show him our need. She also turns to us so that we will open ourselves to Jesus. She said to the servants: "Do whatever he tells you." She did not begin to give orders herself. Many people have a certain anxiety that if we listen to Mary, we will listen less to Jesus. But Mary never points to herself. She always points away from herself to Jesus. She does as the Father does, who at the Transfiguration urges us to "Listen to him" (Mt 17:5). The one who follows Jesus comes to the Father. In the Litany of Loreto we call her *Mater boni concilii*, the "Mother of Good Counsel". Mary gives us good counsel, and her counsel is always this in some form: "Do whatever he tells you." She leads us into a deeper faith and a more total obedience to Jesus.

Jesus performed miracles. He alone. He did it in a way that was completely unexpected. He did not conjure up wine from heaven by magic, but, rather, he allowed what was ordinary to become part of the miracle. He used everything according to its nature. His miracles were not a new creation, but a transformation. In the transformation of water into wine, Jesus already foresaw the transformation of wine into his Blood. Only the one who takes the small, ordinary things seriously can see God's miracles in precisely the ordinary. Perhaps that is where the difficulty lies. And that is also where we need Mary's help. It was probably with a certain hesitation that the servants in Cana began to do what appeared to be such a meaningless task as to fill six gigantic stone jars with water. If Mary, with her own gentle, convincing manner, had not persuaded them to show an initial trust in Jesus, they would never have obeyed such an unreasonable command. It demands faith, at least a beginning of faith, to see God's miracles. God's wonders do not usually satisfy our desire for the sensational; instead, they teach us to show a great respect for the ordinary and to discover that everything small is great. Water can become wine, and wine can become blood.

A Crescendo

"You have kept the good wine until now", said the steward. A truly prophetic word. When God is the one who is acting, the result is always positive. It begins with a little seed, and the seed becomes a tall tree. It begins with water and ends with the Blood of Christ. God wants us to look ahead. The future is always richer than the past. For a Christian, nothing could be as unreasonable as sadly to relive old memories and think back with melancholy on the carefree joy one experienced as a child. A Christian can always say to God: "You have kept the good wine until now." A Christian lives in a constant crescendo.

The account of the wedding feast at Cana teaches us, among many other things, that it is easier to live in this kind of crescendo when we listen to Mary. It is then that she lends us her ears, so that we can better hear and do whatever Jesus tells us.

9

Mary at the Foot of the Cross

Now the hour, which had not yet come at Cana, had finally come. Namely, the hour when Jesus would leave this world and go to the Father and give a total proof of his love (Jn 13:1). Just as Mary was there at Cana when the hour was anticipated, she would also be there when the hour finally arrived. "Standing by the cross of Jesus [was] his mother" (Jn 19:25).

The New Eve

Now Jesus had in truth become the Lamb of God who bore the sins of the world. "For our sake he made him to be sin who knew no sin" (2 Cor 5:21). All of mankind's turning away from God was now concentrated in him, causing him to cry out: "My God, my God, why have you forsaken me?" (Mt 27:46).

Have we ever tried to meditate on Jesus' experience of abandonment by God and considered into what kind of abyss of misery and despair he had descended? No human being had ever been so intimately united with God that he could say: I am God. On the Cross, this bond with God was brutally severed, or, better said, the bond that united him with God was no longer visible for Jesus. We often speak about alienation, but our alienation is only a shadow of what Jesus experienced on the Cross. He became totally foreign to himself. His human nature no longer knew the divine Person who bore this nature. He lived in a kind of "schizophrenia", the tragedy of which no one can imagine. He was like a sea whose water had emptied out: a terrible abyss that shouted to heaven to be filled. The sea of divinity had dried up and was empty. There he showed his love for the Father from the negative side: an endless burning thirst that could not be quenched by anything other than the lost love itself.[1] At the same time, everything he had done during his life was deprived of its meaning. Without God, everything becomes absurd.

In that tragic moment, Mary was there with Jesus. Just as Adam and Eve destroyed God's work of creation together, so Jesus and Mary restored it together. Not that Jesus did a part and Mary did a part. Mary's role consisted in *letting everything happen*. The Second Vatican Council writes: "The Blessed Virgin advanced in her pilgrimage of faith, and faithfully persevered in her union with her Son unto the cross, where she stood, in keeping with the divine plan [cf. Jn 19:25], grieving exceedingly with her only begotten Son, uniting herself with a maternal heart with His sacrifice, and lovingly consenting to the immolation of this Victim

---

[1] Cf. Hans Urs von Balthasar, *The Grain of Wheat: Aphorisms*, trans. Erasmo Leiva-Merikakis (San Francisco: Ignatius Press, 1995), 72.

which she herself had brought forth."[2] She was drawn by her Son into his own obedience to the Father. When she pronounced her "let it be to me according to your word" at the Annunciation, she did not know what that answer would entail. She could not imagine in what kind of adventure she had engaged herself. She had no foresight of the sacrifice she made to God in that Yes. It was only gradually, as the events took place, that she discovered the extent of her first response. Here her Yes reached its utmost limits, or, rather, all the borders were exceeded. She was led into an ocean of suffering.

Mary stood near the Cross like a priest who celebrates Mass: she offered her Son to the Father. That Son whom the Father gave into her hands she gave back freely. The sacrifice that the priest offers in the Eucharist Mary offered at the foot of the Cross. And even if Jesus was the only true High Priest, who "entered once for all into the Holy Place, taking not the blood of goats and calves but his own blood" (Heb 9:12), even if it is this "eternal priesthood" (Heb 7:11–28) which is realized in the Church's priests, Mary stood behind it with her Yes. Without her Yes beneath the Cross, there would be no Eucharist.

All Christians, and priests in particular, should look to Mary to know how to celebrate the Mass. Mary is so one with her Son that she can do nothing but offer

[2] Second Vatican Council, Dogmatic Constitution on the Church *Lumen Gentium*, November 21, 1964, no. 58 (hereafter abbreviated *LG*).

herself when she offers him. Every pain in his body had
a corresponding echo in her heart. And finally, when
his heart was pierced with a lance, she understood
Simeon's prophecy of the sword that would pierce her
own heart. A priest who enters into the school of Mary
knows that he cannot celebrate the Eucharist without
being involved in what he does in total earnest. He cannot offer Christ without offering himself. The Church
has always known that. "Accept from the holy people
of God the gifts to be offered to him. Know what
you are doing, and imitate the mystery you celebrate;
model your life on the mystery of the Lord's cross",
the bishop exhorts the newly ordained priest when he
hands him the paten and the chalice.

"A Fitting Helper for Him"

Jesus said to Mary: "Woman, behold, your son!" (Jn
19:26). As he had done at Cana, Jesus addressed her
with the unusual term "woman". Mary was led into
a universality that shattered the personal mother-son
relationship. Jesus invited her to distance herself from
him as Son in order to become his bride. What had
begun at Cana reached its fulfillment here. Just as the
first woman was given to the man as a "helper" who
was fitting for him (Gen 2:20), so Mary was given
to Jesus as his helper at the foot of the Cross. And
just as the first woman was taken from the side of the
man (Gen 2:23), so Mary was taken from her Son:
everything that she is and has she received from him,

in whom everything was made. From creation to the Cross, it has come full circle.

For Mary to lose her Son was a source of new sufferings for her. She suffered, not merely from seeing her Son suffer, but because she, like Jesus, underwent an immeasurable loss. She suffered from seeing Jesus abandoned by his Father, and she suffered from going through a similar abandonment. Both of them lost everything: Jesus his Father, and Mary her Son. Mary is the New Eve not only because she endured abandonment by God with him. With good reason the holy Church Fathers realized that Mary was not used as a purely passive instrument; rather, she cooperated with free faith and obedience in the salvation of mankind.[3] By voluntarily losing her Son, she showed her deepest solidarity with him who had himself lost his Father. Precisely by being separated from her Son, she was most intimately united with him. The bond of love between them was so strong that it could never bear any separation. The bond could be stretched and strained to the extreme. Still, it would not break. Who loves the most: the one who wishes to be always with the beloved or the one who, out of love for the beloved, is willing to renounce being with him?

Mother of the Church

Jesus gave Mary to John: "Behold, your Mother." John represented the Church and, in the end, all of mankind.

---

[3] *LG* 56.

Jesus distanced himself from his Mother and gave her to the Church. And Mary distanced herself from her Son and placed herself completely at the Church's disposal.

It cannot be a matter of indifference that we, the Church, have received Mary as our Mother. It is not something we can accept or reject according to our own good pleasure. To disown one's mother always has disastrous consequences. The reaction of John was that "from that hour the disciple took her to his own home" (Jn 19:27). When Pope Paul VI proclaimed Mary Mother of the Church after the Second Vatican Council, this was only a confirmation of a reality the Church had been living during her entire history, a history that began at the foot of the Cross. When John invited Mary to live with him, it was the Church that acknowledged Mary as her Mother.

John had an impulsive temperament. Jesus called him and his brother James "Boanerges", sons of thunder (Mk 3:17). When the Samaritans refused to take Jesus in, these two sons of Zebedee said: "Lord, do you want us to bid fire come down from heaven and consume them?" (Lk 9:54). John needed to change a great deal before he was mature enough to write his letters about love. He would perhaps never have been the apostle of love and, with Saint Paul, the great theologian of the early Church if Mary, in her discreet way, had not come to his aid. Without a doubt, her motherly tenderness and gentleness contributed greatly in melting the hardness of his heart afterward.

She raised Jesus and formed his heart, so that later he could say of himself: "I am gentle and lowly in heart" (Mt 11:29). She surely took up her work again day after day and fashioned John after the heart of Jesus. The name Boanerges was quickly forgotten, probably because it was no longer suitable for the fundamentally transformed John. When he later spoke of himself, he gave himself a name that was completely the opposite of "son of thunder": "the disciple whom Jesus loved".

We can try to imagine what tenderness and joy Mary and John must have experienced in each others' company. How often they must have conversed about Jesus; Mary perhaps mostly listening to what John told her about those two years when he walked the dusty streets of Palestine with Jesus. During these long, intimate discussions, a clearer insight grew in Mary and John about all that Jesus had said and done. Is it so remarkable that his Gospel possesses a special depth and that the mystics have always had a preference for it?

"Unless you turn and become like children, you will never enter the kingdom of heaven" (Mt 18:3). Why do we always wish to be so grown up, so adult? Why do we want to carry all our sorrows alone? Why not let ourselves be comforted by her whom we call "comforter of the afflicted"? Our relationship to the Father in heaven, and to Mary our Mother, gives us a unique chance to let the child hidden deep within us be expressed.

We could analyze the mother-child relationship and thus show how our relationship should be to Mary.

But on one point the comparison would not hold. The mother often dies before her child. She is not there when her child makes that great leap. Mary, on the other hand, is always there, "now and at the hour of our death". At that moment, when one's whole life receives its final meaning, Mary is more present than ever. No one needs to cross the threshold alone. When we die, Mary takes us by the hand, and, with our hand in hers, we make our entrance into heaven. What a joy when she "shows us Jesus, the blessed fruit of her womb, when this earthly exile is ended!" (*Salve Regina*).

During the war [World War II], I was a novice in Brygge. The day after the city's liberation by the Canadian troops, one of our fathers came home with a helmet that had belonged to a fallen German soldier. His dead body had been left by the Germans. In the inner pocket of the uniform, one of my brothers in the Order had found a letter the soldier had received from his mother. I remember with what reverence we took the letter in our hands and tried to decipher the writing, the difficult Fraktur letters that were still used by the Germans at the time. At that moment none of us thought this soldier was an enemy. Apart from the political relations and the war, we also felt concretely that he was his mother's child, someone who loved his mother and who was loved by her. We felt a bond with her and her fallen son.

The memory of a mother's love brings people closer to each other. The thought of her is capable of breaking down dividing walls. The mother has a mysterious gift of creating unity instead of division, love instead of hate. If we long for the unity of Christ's Church, we cannot leave Mary outside. The mother is the harmonious bond in the home.

10

Mary and the Holy Spirit

In one of the most beautiful statements about Mary, the council explains that she is "fashioned by the Holy Spirit" (*Quasi a Spiritu Sancto plasmata*).[1] She is a work of art designed by the Holy Spirit. A masterpiece that bears witness to the Artist. To honor Mary is to worship the Holy Spirit, for everything that Mary is and has is a fruit of his work. It cannot be an accident that Mary is called *Advocata nostra*, in the liturgy, exactly the same name Jesus gave to the Holy Spirit (*Paraklētos*). The Orthodox call Mary *Panagia* (all holy). Mary cannot hide her origin. She is humble and works in hiddenness, like the Holy Spirit; he who does not even have a name of his own ("Spirit" is a name that applies to the whole Godhead: "God is spirit" [Jn 4:24]) and whose entire mission consists in revealing the Father through Jesus.

[1] *LG* 56.

The "Motherly" Mission of the Spirit and Mary

Mary could never have been the Mother of Jesus and our Mother if the Holy Spirit had not let her share in his own "motherly" function. It has often been pointed out that the Holy Spirit acts as a mother. We read as early as the Book of Genesis that the Spirit was "hovering over" the waters (English Standard Version, 1:2), as a hen that sits and broods on her eggs. (The image is from Gregory Nazianzen [329–389]). "It is the Spirit that gives life", Jesus says (Jn 6:63). And "unless one is born of water and the Spirit, he cannot enter the kingdom of God" (Jn 3:5). In our Creed we call the Spirit "the Giver of Life". Is it not the joy of a mother to teach the child to say "papa?" In the same way, the Spirit teaches us to say "Abba! Father!" (Rom 8:15). The Pentecost sequence gives us a detailed description of the Spirit's motherly role: he comforts in sorrow, gives relief in sickness, he cleans what is soiled, heals what is wounded, and softens what is hardened. All of this can also be said of Mary. It is Mary who is the sign of the Spirit's motherly love on earth. Something essential in God would not have become visible and concrete for us if Mary had not existed. Saint Maximilian Kolbe dares to say that Mary is, in a certain way, the incarnation of the Holy Spirit.[2] He immediately

[2] Cf. H. M. Manteau-Bonamy, O.P., *Immaculate Conception and*

adds, of course, that the Holy Spirit is not incarnated, but "in some way" he nevertheless becomes visible thanks to Mary. There is nothing in her that does not point to the Holy Spirit.

Saint Maximilian Kolbe sees in Mary's Immaculate Conception a replica of the uncreated Immaculate Conception who is the Holy Spirit. "And who is the Holy Spirit?" he asks. "The flowering of the love of the Father and the Son. If the fruit of created love is a created conception, then the fruit of divine Love, that prototype of all created love, is necessarily a divine 'conception.' The Holy Spirit is, therefore, the 'uncreated eternal conception,' the prototype of all the conceptions that multiply life throughout the whole universe."[3] Kolbe was surprised by Mary's answer to Bernadette. "In her apparition at Lourdes she does not say: 'I was conceived immaculately'; but 'I am the Immaculate Conception.' This points up not only the fact that she was conceived without sin, but also the manner in which this privilege belongs to her. It is not something accidental; it is something that belongs to her very nature."[4] Mary, like the Holy Spirit, points to the fruitful power of love. Her being is a living

---

the Holy Spirit, The Marian Teachings of Fr. Kolbe, rev. ed. (Libertyville, Ill.: Marytown Press, 2008), 41. Maximilian Kolbe, born 1894, died in 1941 in a concentration camp in Auschwitz, where he freely offered his life to save a fellow prisoner. Declared blessed in 1971, and canonized a saint in 1982.

[3] Ibid., 17.

[4] Ibid., 7.

revelation of what love can bring about. She reminds us in our day that in order for love to be true, it must be open. The Holy Spirit shows in the Trinity that the love of the Father and the Son is not an "égoïsme-à-deux"; rather, it bears fruit. In the same way, by *being* the Immaculate Conception, Mary shows that nothing is so foreign to love as sterility. Mary's whole being is a song of praise to the fruitfulness of love. It should not surprise us that in her liturgy the Church calls her "a garden locked" (Song 4:12). The Church takes the admiring words of the Bridegroom in her mouth: "Your shoots are an orchard of pomegranates with all choicest fruits . . . with all trees of frankincense, myrrh and aloes, with all chief spices" (Song 4:13–14). Mary is truly "Alma Mater" (fruitful mother). Wherever she is and works, there new life begins to grow.

The council calls Mary "the temple of the Holy Spirit".[5] The Holy Spirit is given to every Christian (Rom 5:5), but never was he so at home in any person —apart from Jesus—as he was in Mary. She bore him, not as a lifeless treasure, but rather as a living spring that freely welled up inside of her. Yes, he filled her so that he penetrated all the pores of her being. When the Spirit set about his gigantic task of renewing the face of the earth (Ps 104:30), he began with Mary. He did his work so fundamentally in her that it can be a model for all that is to follow. The cosmic music the Spirit wants to call forth from creation reached its peak once and

[5] *LG* 53.

for all in the music he drew forth from Mary. "Awake, O harp and lyre! I will awake the dawn!" the Spirit said to Mary (Ps 57:8). And she immediately began to make music and bring forth light. She is the only instrument that always produced the exact melody the Spirit intended. All other instruments, at least sometimes, play flat notes. Mary, on the other hand, made perfect music throughout her entire life. She was always in perfect harmony with the Spirit.

Mary's Pentecost

Mary's relationship to the Spirit is marked by an unimaginable dynamism. Moment by moment she grew into him and he into her. It began with her conception in her mother's womb. Even then she was completely in the Spirit's power. Nothing within her evaded the Spirit's influence. Because everything in her said a wholehearted Yes to him, he could have recourse to her with absolute freedom and prepare her for the mission for which she was created: to be the Mother of God and of mankind. We cannot imagine how quickly a person is sanctified and divinized when there is no doubt, not even a shadow of a No in her; when all her powers are mobilized and concentrated on the one thing necessary. Saint Ignatius of Loyola believed that few could realize what God would do with them if they wished to surrender to the inspiration of grace without reservation; if they distanced themselves from themselves and completely surrendered to the Divine

Master, so that he could form their souls between his hands.[6]

Every moment in Mary's life meant crossing a threshold. Not a single moment was like another. But there were certainly some thresholds that were more important and more decisive than others. The Annunciation was one of them. When the Spirit overshadowed her, she became "full of grace" in a completely new way, or, rather, her being expanded so that she could contain him in whom "the whole fullness of deity dwells" (Col 2:9).

Pentecost was the other decisive threshold. It was also decisive for the disciples, but Mary's situation was unique. As long as Jesus was living, the disciples could not receive the Holy Spirit (cf. Jn 16:7).

The Spirit had not yet been given, writes John (7:39). He really says it with much greater force: there was not yet any Spirit. And still, in Mary he was there. All of his power was gathered and concentrated in her. In contrast to the apostles, she was already familiar with the Spirit. The council states: "We see . . . before the day of Pentecost . . . Mary the Mother of Jesus . . . by her prayers imploring the gift of the Spirit, who had already overshadowed her in the Annunciation."[7] But the Spirit comes now with a new mission for her. At the Annunciation the Spirit made her Mother of God's Son; at Pentecost he made her Mother of the

[6] Ignatius of Loyola, 1491–1556. Cf. Bengt Ingmar Kilström and Lars Rooth, in *Jesu sällskap, Skeab* (Stockholm, 1979), 194.
[7] LG 59.

Church, and more than that: he made her an archetype of the Church. Saint Luke brings out the meaning of Mary's presence among the disciples by explicitly mentioning her "together with the women" (Acts 1:14). It was surely Mary who was praying and longing the most among the many who were gathered in the upper room where the disciples usually stayed. Though she was already filled with the Spirit, she felt she was the one who had the greatest need of receiving still more of him. For her own sake or for the sake of the Church? The question is meaningless. She is the center of the Church, and everything she received, she received for the sake of the Church.

Pentecost is the official birthday of the Church. The Church was already born in a hidden way at the foot of the Cross when Jesus gave Mary to John and John to Mary and when water and blood flowed out of his pierced side. The Church Fathers have often pointed out that the sacraments, in particular baptism and the Eucharist, poured forth from the heart of Jesus in a mystical way and that the Church was born from the open side of Jesus as Eve was formed from the rib of Adam (Gen 2:21:22). But what happened in a hidden and subtle way beneath the Cross became clear and active at Pentecost. Beneath the Cross, the child was born, but on Pentecost he began to speak. We can imagine Mary standing in the midst of the disciples filled with the Holy Spirit and speaking in tongues more than all the others. She showed that her silence was transformed into a holy jubilation when she sang

her *Magnificat* as soon as the Spirit began to play on
the strings. Mary was surely the first to begin speaking in the Spirit, and her overflowing jubilation later
took hold of the disciples, so that they in their turn
began to speak as though they were "filled with new
wine" (Acts 2:13). In the Church, everything happens, or ought to happen, from inside out. Mary is
the Church's center. Everything she received was in
overflowing measure because it was meant not merely
for her, but for all.

Mary and Peter

Even though Mary is the center of the Church, nevertheless we see that it is Peter who takes the lead and
begins to speak to the people about Jesus. Mary has
a special relationship to Peter. Both of them have responsibility for the *whole* Church. The apostles receive
a distinct area where the Gospel shall be proclaimed.
But Peter becomes shepherd of the whole flock (Jn
21:15–17). He receives power to bind and loose (Mt
16:19). Mary is also responsible for the whole Church,
but in another way than Peter. Peter represents the office; Mary is unity and love. By her motherly influence, she tempers and softens the strict objectivity of
the hierarchy. Peter is the Church's infallibility; Mary
is her holiness. When the Holy Spirit is poured out
over Mary and the disciples at Pentecost, he conse-
crates them all to their vocations. Peter is the rock on

which the Church is built; Mary is the womb from which she was born.

When we say that Mary is the Mother of Jesus, it means more than that she gave birth to Jesus in Bethlehem. She is the Mother of the whole Christ, of his whole Body, which will eventually be built up in love (cf. Eph 4:16). At Pentecost, her motherhood becomes universalized. Jesus, who became universally present in the whole Church through his Spirit, at the same time gave Mary, his Bride, a worldwide dimension. Her womb encompasses the Church in such a way that no one can leave it. We are always *in sinu matris* (in the mother's womb).

II

The Assumption of Mary

Mary's Assumption into heaven need not be interpreted to mean she did not die. We can think of Mary,
who imitated her Son in everything, as also experienc-
ing death in some way. How could she have gone another way than he did? How could God have deprived
her of what all the saints have desired, to "share his sufferings, becoming like him in his death" (Phil 3:10). It
is true, death is a consequence of sin, but Jesus transformed it into a possibility of the utmost importance.
Since Jesus "with a loud voice" cried out: "Father, into
your hands I commit my spirit!" (Lk 23:46), Christian
death has become a final, all-embracing act of surrender. At the moment of death, man receives the possibility of gathering his whole life and placing it irre-
vocably into God's hands. Death is like pronouncing
a vow, not with words, but in action and in "dead"
earnest, to belong to him for all eternity. We can be
sure that Mary did not lose this final opportunity.

Therefore, we can learn from Mary how to die.
Above all, we can learn that death is an art we can practice our entire life. Mary's unceasing Yes was a way
of leaving herself to "go to the Father" (Jn 14:28),

which is the Christian definition of death. When one
has died countless times during one's life, what we
call "death" is transformed into an "assumption into
heaven". This is perhaps one of the most important
things the Assumption can teach us.

Taken up into Heaven

The Church believes that Mary was assumed body and
soul into heaven, that is, with her whole personality.
Just as Jesus did not leave his body in the grave after
his death to return as a pure spirit to the Father but,
rather, took his body with him to allow it to share
forever in God's glory, so Mary's body was also taken
into heaven. What Jesus says to his disciples after the
Resurrection: "A spirit has not flesh and bones as you
see that I have" (Lk 24:39), Mary also says to us: "I
am not a ghost, I am a human being like you—and I
am in heaven."

The question of life after death has concerned mankind since the beginning of time. What happens to
man after death? Is his life definitively finished when
he dies? Is he no more than a creature who appears for
a brief moment on the horizon of time, only to disap-
pear immediately afterward? Or is he doomed to live
many lives, as certain Asian religions maintain, in order
finally to be dissolved into the divine all? Or does man
become freed at death from the body in order to live
on as a pure spirit? What the Church teaches about
Mary gives us a concrete insight into what life after

death will be. Nothing of Mary's personality has been lost. Her entire being has been transported to heaven. The old is not destroyed but transformed. Mary is, and remains, for all eternity a human being, but a glorified one.

This is not a destiny that concerns Mary alone. As Mother of the new mankind, she shows what all of us may hope for. Every person who dies in the love of God will be taken up to heaven, not with half of his being, but with his whole personality.

Should it surprise us that not only Mary's soul but also her body has been taken into heaven? She had, of course, offered herself entirely to God. At the Annunciation, she placed her body at the disposal of the Holy Spirit, and it became a temple of God when the Spirit overshadowed her. The Spirit was at work in her throughout her whole life, and when she reached the end of her life, she was seized by the irresistible power of the Spirit and, in a divine hurricane, so to speak, was drawn up to heaven (2 Kings 2:11).

But our body is also a temple of the Holy Spirit and also stands at God's disposal (1 Cor 6:19). Our body is also made holy by the sacraments and, above all, by being in contact with the Body and Blood of Christ. Therefore our body will also, at some point, be taken up to heaven. Nothing that is offered to God is lost. Everything is taken up and transformed.

A New Presence

Mary's Assumption into heaven does not mean that she traveled away to a far distant land. We imagine heaven to be "up there". "Glory to God in the highest", we sing in the Gloria. It is not wrong to have this conception, as long as we realize it does not completely convey the reality. Heaven is not a place that lies beyond the limits of the universe, but a dimension we cannot perceive with our earthly senses. Because Mary has been taken up into heaven, she has not therefore left us. Quite the contrary. For that very reason she has penetrated more deeply into the world.

As long as Mary lived in her mortal body, she was bound by time and space. She could not be present in more than one place at a time. When she lived with John after Jesus' Resurrection, she prayed earnestly for the new Church, but she could not be present when the apostles went out to proclaim the Gospel. But after her Assumption into heaven, all the borders burst, and her whole being, including her body, was glorified. A glorified body has no definite contours. It can be present in different places at the same time and take on cosmic dimensions. Through Mary's Assumption, she passed over to a universal presence from the limited presence that characterized her life on earth. Always and everywhere Mary is with us, wherever we may be and wherever we may go. She fills the whole universe. She is "clothed with the sun, with the moon under her feet, and on her head a crown of twelve stars" (Rev

12:1). When we pray the "Hail Mary" during the day, on the street or at work, we do not speak into a vacuum. Mary is always present. It can give us great joy to discover that Mary's Assumption into heaven, which appeared to take her far away, really brought her closer to us. Thanks to the Assumption, she is present at the center of our lives.

Neither should we think Mary is in heaven to enjoy undisturbed peace. As long as the fight between light and darkness continues, Mary is involved. We know that Jesus "always lives to make intercession for [us]" (Heb 7:25), that he goes to "prepare a place for [us]" (Jn 14:2). But he does not do it without his "helper" (cf. Gen 2:20). Even in heaven, Mary lives only for her Son and his redemptive work.

The Church's Assumption

There has always been a mysterious tension between heaven and earth. The tension is apparent in the first words of the Bible. "In the beginning God created the heavens and the earth" (Gen 1:1). Heaven is the place where God lives, while earth is the dwelling place of men. God indeed never intended the opposition to be as great as it actually became. We read that the Lord God walked in the garden of paradise in the cool of the evening (Gen 3:8). But the Fall separated heaven and earth by a great abyss (cf. Lk 16:26).

In the fullness of time, however, God came down to earth. His descending made heaven visible and tangibly present on earth. "He who has seen me has seen the

Father" (Jn 14:9). Heaven was in our midst in Jesus as a You who could love and be loved. He died for man, and, when he was dead, heaven also disappeared. He descended into the heart of the earth (Mt 12:40) in order to enter completely into the hidden roots of things and to draw the whole earth with him when he ascended again to his Father. When Jesus ascended into heaven, he did not ascend alone. The whole earth was taken to heaven.[1] This gave our longing for heaven a particular stamp: we do not long for something that lies in the future. No, we long for something that already *is* but that we cannot see, due to the veil covering our eyes. Since Jesus took us with him when he ascended into heaven, we are all citizens of heaven (Phil 3:20) and, therefore, strangers and exiles on earth (Heb 11:13).

In principle we have already gone to heaven, but since we do not live wholeheartedly as Christians, we are in practice often far away from it. Nevertheless, the principle is not merely an abstraction. It has become a concrete reality in Mary. Mary's Assumption into heaven is also our assumption. Mary represents in herself the whole Church and, ultimately, all of mankind. When the Church sings every Sunday at Vespers "The marriage of the Lamb has come, and his Bride has made herself ready" (Rev 19:7), the bride is at the same time both Mary and the Church. Mary and the Church are

---

[1] Cf. Hans Urs von Balthasar, *Prayer*, trans. Graham Harrison (San Francisco: Ignatius Press, 1986), 278-79.

inseparable. The Bride is united with her Bridegroom by the fact that Mary was assumed into heaven, and so the heavenly wedding feast has already begun. The Bride longs so impatiently for the Bridegroom that she cannot wait until the end of time. And the Bridegroom himself longs for the Bride. "I will come again and will take you to myself, that where I am you may be also" (Jn 14:3). He does not wish to wait any longer to celebrate the wedding: "Everything is ready; come to the marriage feast!" (Mt 22:4). By Mary's Assumption we have come. The wedding feast no longer belongs to the future, it is a reality *now*.

Here again we can see how God cannot resist anticipating the final realities. God cannot wait. He arranges things so that the reality, even though it comes about after a long period of time, is nevertheless in some way already present from the beginning. In baptism man dies to sin and rises up out of the water created anew and dripping with divine life. And his whole life is directed toward fulfilling this reality that was already there from the beginning. The Eucharist is heaven come down to earth. In it man may nourish himself with the Bread of Angels, even though he lives an earthly existence. God always makes things complete, but we need an entire lifetime to become conscious of what has already taken place. God creates so that the goal is there from the beginning. The goal is not only the last, but also the first. The account of paradise in the Book of Genesis corresponds to the description of heaven in the Book of Revelation. All that has been written between the first and last page of the Bible, and all that is fought out and experienced from the beginning of history to its end, is nothing more than an attempt to integrate the reality that has always existed in its fundamental outline.

We do not need to exert great effort to achieve something that does not yet exist. It is more a question of resting in what we have already received. The heavenly Jerusalem is a reality now, not a one-sided masculine reality (through the Ascension of Christ), but fully human as man *and* woman. Since Mary has been assumed into heaven, the goal for which we all strive is in a certain way already attained.

The Dogma Defined

Mary's Assumption was proclaimed a dogma by Pope Pius XII on November 1, 1950. That is to say, the pope, in the power of his authority as universal shepherd of the Church, defined that Mary's Assumption is a truth of faith revealed by God. On a questionnaire to the bishops, 98 percent answered that they considered the dogma to be timely and possible. The pope referred to Genesis 3:15, which has traditionally been interpreted by the Church as Mary's absolute victory over Satan. (Vulgate: *Ipsa* conteret caput tuum: *She* shall crush your head.) Farther on, the pope cited the Gospels, where Mary stands out as intimately united with her Son. Such a bond cannot be limited to life on earth but must also characterize even her heavenly existence.

The biblical arguments would in themselves be insufficient if the Assumption of Mary into heaven had not been a generally recognized article of faith in the Church for many centuries. Mary's Assumption has been celebrated solemnly since the eighth century. The Church is conscious of the fact that under the inspiration of the Holy Spirit, she is gradually led into "all the truth" (Jn 16:13), which is much greater than one can realize at a first, superficial reading of individual texts. Because the Church treasures God's Word and ponders it in her heart (Lk 2:19), she eventually arrives at a deeper level. God's Word is so inscrutable that it needs hundreds of years of meditation of an entire Church to search out its riches.

Many wonder if the dogma defined in 1950 caused perhaps more harm than good for the Church. Does it not place a new obstacle in the way of reunification of the churches? Perhaps. But we can also see the proclamation of this dogma from another perspective. Could God not have arranged that the Church, at the last minute, so to speak, just before mankind—thus also the Church—was afflicted by the worst crisis in its history, would receive a final opportunity to make more clear than ever the great dignity of man? Mary's Assumption reveals what God has thought about man and what he has planned for him. The one who looks at Mary knows that, despite everything, there is a future for man. Yes, he understands that the future and the present are not as distinguishable as they might seem, but that they, in a mysterious way, flow into each other. When we read in Saint Paul: "Those whom he called he also justified; and those whom he justified he also glorified" (Rom 8:30), we cannot help but think of Mary. But the apostle's words apply also to us. Our glory has already begun, because Mary has paved the way and lives glorified now with body and soul in heaven. Her glory is our glory: "You are the exaltation of Jerusalem, you are the great glory of Israel, you are the great pride of our nation!" (Jud 15:9).

12

Mary and the Church

What the world has most need of is meaning and security. The crisis of our day stems from having lost contact with the whole. Man no longer feels a part of something greater and all-encompassing, where he has a clear place and finds his identity. He has lost meaning and a sense of belonging and feels he is moving about without a plan. The neurosis we find today is due no longer to a repression of sexuality but much more to the fact that the threads connecting man to his roots have been severed. When God no longer exists or is no longer acknowledged as Father, then we are no longer brothers and sisters. Instead of siblings, we become "fellowmen". By placing the emphasis on a "self-realization" that is seen in an individualistic way, we have become a kind of "monad" (Leibniz) without doors or windows. Though man is created as a limb in a body, he acts as though he were the whole body. But since "no man is an island", it is not surprising he feels anguish and meaninglessness as a little island.

A Masculine Church?

We would have expected the Church to give man
something to live for, to fulfill his basic need for meaning and a sense of belonging. Instead, it seems ever
more people are leaving the Church. They no longer
experience the Church as their home

Why is that so? One reason may be that the Church
has become all too masculine. "The Church since the
Council", writes Hans Urs von Balthasar, "has to a
large extent put off her mystical characteristics; she
has become a Church of permanent conversations,
organizations, advisory commissions, congresses, syn-
ods, commissions, academies, parties, pressure groups,
functions, structures and restructurings, sociological
experiments, statistics: that is to say, more than ever a
male Church. . . . May not the reason for the domi-
nation of such typically male and abstract notions be
because of the abandonment of the deep femininity of
the marian character of the Church?"[1] The Church
has always been considered the great Mother, *Mater
Ecclesia*. But only when she is faithful to her feminine
nature can she regain her power to draw in new mem-
bers, and then, in the future, the wavering and home-
less will also find warmth and security in her embrace.

---

[1] Hans Urs von Balthasar, *Elucidations*, trans. John Riches (San
Francisco: Ignatius Press, 1998), 109–10.

Mary, Archetype of the Church

The Church is not an abstract feminine figure. In Mary she has become concrete. Mary is often only considered a symbol of the Church due to certain parallels between them both. But Mary is more. She is, as the Second Vatican Council says: "hailed as preeminent and . . . its type and excellent exemplar".[2] It is true Mary is an individual human person and as such a member of the Church, but she can at the same time be said to be the Church herself, because she is her innermost heart. Just as in man there is a mysterious spring in his depths where he has direct contact with heaven and where he is at the same time most himself, so there is also in the Church a kernel that is heavenly and without which she would lose her form. The Church is more than Mary, but in Mary the Church is most herself.

Many of the Church Fathers have pointed out that Mary and the Church are reflected in each other. When we wish to know how the Church should be, and already is in her innermost center, we need only look at Mary. When the Church has recourse to her as Queen of Apostles, Martyrs, Virgins . . . , it is because the very substance of apostleship, martyrdom, and virginity, and so on, is found in a perfect way in Mary.

[2] *LG* 53.

Every saint has his place in the Church: he has a definite work or task and has a limited sphere of influence. Mary, on the other hand, has her place at the center of the Church, as the heart in the body, and therefore her radiance reaches all. While the saints are lamps, Mary is the sun. And the Book of Revelation even shows her clothed with the sun (12:1).

Pope Paul VI officially granted her the title: *Mater Ecclesiae* (Mother of the Church). It should be a reflex with us to turn our gaze to Mary when we think of the Church. Mary is Mother of the Church because she gave birth to Christ, who as her head is united with the whole body and her limbs. But at the same time Mary stands opposite Christ as his chosen Bride "without spot or wrinkle" (Eph 5:27). When John sees "the holy city, new Jerusalem, coming down out of heaven from God, prepared as a bride adorned for her husband" (Rev 21:2), these words about the Church receive their full weight only when we consider Mary, who is the innermost center of the Church. Only in her is the Church "adorned". In her she has already reached her perfection.

Meditating on Mary is also always meditating on the Church, and vice-versa. For us in the West, who have a tendency to reduce the Church to a system or an organization, it is vital to see her personified in Mary. Mary is Mother and Virgin, and so also is the Church.

> For in the mystery of the Church, which is itself rightly called mother and virgin, the Blessed Virgin

stands out in eminent and singular fashion as exemplar both of virgin and mother. By her belief and obedience, not knowing man but overshadowed by the Holy Spirit, as the new Eve she brought forth on earth the very Son of the Father, showing an undefiled faith, not in the word of the ancient serpent, but in that of God's messenger. The Son whom she brought forth is He whom God placed as the first-born among many brethren, namely, the faithful, in whose birth and education she cooperates with a maternal love. The Church indeed, contemplating her hidden sanctity, imitating her charity and faithfully fulfilling the Father's will, by receiving the word of God in faith becomes herself a mother. By her preaching she brings forth to a new and immortal life the sons who are born to her in baptism, conceived of the Holy Spirit and born of God. She herself is a virgin, who keeps the faith given to her by her Spouse whole and entire. Imitating the mother of her Lord, and by the power of the Holy Spirit, she keeps with virginal purity an entire faith, a firm hope and a sincere charity.[3]

Unceasingly Mary presents an ideal for the Church, in which the contradiction between virginity and motherhood is overcome. Everyone in the Church who promises virginity knows that when they look to Mary their lives do not become sterile, but, on the contrary, they receive a new fruitfulness. Just as Mary, thanks to her total openness to the Holy Spirit, could give birth

[3] *LG* 63–64.

to a child who was "the Son of God" (Lk 1:35), so also, these children to whom virginity gives birth in the Church are "born not of blood nor of the will of the flesh nor of the will of man, but of God" (Jn 1:13). The virginity and fruitfulness of the Church live not only in those who make a vow of virginity. Even those in the married state, who recognize the covenant between Christ and the Church (Eph 5:32), bear witness to the Church's virginity.

If we have a tendency to place too much emphasis on organization and measurable results, we can learn from Mary how to nurture new life: that it happens, not collectively, but through personal contact. Mary prepared Jesus for many years for what the Father was expecting from him. The human heart is not formed on an assembly line but, rather, slowly, patiently, and through personal contact and concrete love. The need for spiritual directors in the Church would not be so glaring if more priests and laity learned from Mary the art of assisting a fellow human being in his growth "in wisdom and in stature" (Lk 2:52).

The Church Is Characterized by Mary

It is the Church's duty to examine herself continually to see if she corresponds with her archetype in attitude and behavior. Mary is the criterion that enables the Church to evaluate if she is still being faithful to her deepest nature. It is not enough that the Church is pure and immaculate in her inmost center.

She is called to be so even to her outer periphery. Every Christian should let his life be characterized by Mary. One is a true *anima ecclesiastica* (soul of the Church) only if Mary's attitude becomes living and concrete in his own heart.

What characterizes Mary's attitude is that she lives for others. In two scenes that follow one another, Saint Luke describes her as the handmaid of the Lord (at the Annunciation) and the handmaid of mankind (at the Visitation to Elizabeth). Each time her service has to do with birth and new life. As "the dwelling of God . . . with men" (Rev 21:3), she is a faithful mirror of the life of the Holy Trinity: just as the three divine Persons flow unceasingly toward and into each other, so Mary flows out to God and men. Nothing in her is private. Everything is at the disposal of everyone. We depart from Mary and become "unlike the Church" (un-Church-like) as soon as we wish to be something for ourselves or carry out our own will. It is probably due to the decline in Marian consciousness in the Church that the world's resistance to obedience has been able to force its way into the Church and threaten to weaken her from within. The widespread criticism and spirit of revolt point to the fact that Mary is no longer living and real for many churchmen. How could disobedience find fertile ground in one who lovingly sought to imitate Mary, whose life was one single, uninterrupted *Yes*?

Only when Mary receives her obvious place again can the Church be completely herself. Most of all in the life of men who respect womanhood in her. In particular, Mary is a shining example and loving Mother for the priest, who has a special responsibility in the Church. In his letter to priests before Holy Thursday 1979, Saint John Paul II underlined that John, who received Mary as his mother at the foot of the Cross, received full authority to celebrate the Holy Eucharist and that therefore the priests who have received the same authority, in a certain sense, are the first to have the right to see in Mary their Mother. And the pope continues: "In the midst of the People of God, that looks to Mary with immense love and hope, you must look to her with exceptional hope and love. Indeed, you must proclaim Christ who is her Son; and who will better communicate to you the truth about him than his Mother? You must nourish human hearts with Christ: and who can make you more aware of what you are doing than she who nourished him? . . . In our 'ministerial' priesthood there is a wonderful penetrating dimension of nearness to the Mother of Christ. So let us try to live in that dimension."

It cannot be so difficult for a woman in the Church to grasp the Church's Marian character. Statistics about the relationship between men and women who attend Church services should show clearly that women feel more at home in the Church than men. A comparison of men and women religious Orders should also make clear that by far more women than men feel called to a life of virginity and wish to make the name *Sponsa Christi* (Bride of Christ) their own, which signifies both Mary and the Church. In her desire to give birth to children, every woman, at the same time, embodies something of the Church's universal motherhood. Since the woman is by nature generally more open than the man, she is also especially receptive to the Holy Spirit, who has overshadowed Mary and given life to the Church. Is it not significant that according to the *Didache* of the apostles (third century), which, among other things, discussed the position of deaconesses in the Church, stated that the bishop represents the Father, the deacon the Son, and the deaconess the Holy Spirit? The woman's special affinity with the Spirit cannot surprise one who knows that the Spirit "unites in love" the Father and the Son in the Holy Trinity. Is the woman, more than the man, not also the bond of love in the family? But she is that only when she dares to be herself and does not try desperately, driven by an unconscious self-contempt, to play the role of the man. If the woman flees her specific responsibility, the Church, like society today, will become one-sidedly masculine and anything but *Mater Ecclesiae*.

An Open Church

At that moment on the Cross when Jesus said to Mary: "Woman, behold, your son!" and to John: "Behold, your mother!" (Jn 19:26–27), the Church came into existence. The charismatic Church, represented by John, was united with the Apostolic Church, and together they formed the whole Church founded by the

Lord and built upon Peter: a Church that is both heavenly and earthly, immaculate and sinful, charismatic and hierarchical. Mary and Peter both have their specific ministries. Jesus entrusted his Church to both. The Church of love and the official Church should exist together in a fruitful and healthy tension, where both keep each other in balance. A one-sided hierarchical Church would be sterile, hard, and formalistic. A one-sided charismatic Church, on the other hand, would lack definite contours. "All things are twofold, one opposite the other" (Sir 42:24).

Does that mean the Church of love is the same as the hierarchical Church? No. To be sure, love is integrated into the official ministry, but not limited to or locked into it. Love is always greater. When Peter, after having been appointed to his office as shepherd of the Church ("feed my sheep!" Jn 21:15-17), asks how it will be for John (who in contrast to Peter represents here the Church of love), Jesus answers: "If it is my will that he remain until I come, what is that to you? Follow me!" (Jn 21:22). This answer seems to give a discreet hint that the borders of the visible Church and the Church of love do not coincide. No ones knows what happens with love. Do not make any theories about it, Jesus says to Peter. Do not search into matters that do not concern you. Do not try to program and direct love, but rather let it go its own ways.

The Gospel of John ends with a question mark. A question mark that remains. No one knows where the Church of love begins and ends. Under Mary's mantle

there is unlimited space. The Vatican Council admits
that we cannot claim that no one can be saved outside the visible, hierarchical Church: "The Christian
. . . linked with the paschal mystery and patterned on
the dying Christ, . . . will hasten forward to resurrection in the strength which comes from hope. All this
holds true not only for Christians, but for all men of
good will in whose hearts grace works in an unseen
way. For, since Christ died for all men, and since the
ultimate vocation of man is in fact one, and divine,
we ought to believe that the Holy Spirit in a manner
known only to God offers to every man the possibility
of being associated with this paschal mystery."[4]

   We may not conclude from this that all religions are
equal paths to salvation. Jesus' command is ever valid:
"Go therefore and make disciples of all nations, bap-
tizing them in the name of the Father and of the Son
and of the Holy Spirit, teaching them to observe all
that I have commanded you" (Mt 28:19–20). It is not
a matter of indifference if one absorbs a few weak rays
or if one stands directly in the sun. But to the one who
asks exactly how many rays are necessary to be saved,
Jesus answers: "What is that to you? Follow me."

----

[4] Second Vatican Council, Pastoral Constitution on the Church
in the Modern World *Gaudium et Spes*, December 7, 1965, no. 22.

13

Our Lady of the Dark Night

"A deeper enlightenment and wider experience than mine is necessary to explain the dark night through which a soul journeys toward that divine light of perfect union with God, which is achieved, insofar as possible in this life, through love. The darknesses and trials, spiritual and temporal, that fortunate souls ordinarily encounter on their way to the high state of perfection are so numerous and profound that human science cannot understand them adequately." With these words Saint John of the Cross begins the first book of *The Ascent of Mount Carmel.*[1]

To Die in Order to Live

The work that God does in a person who turns to him reaches far deeper levels, and is therefore much more painful, than modern day psychoanalysis. In his action, God is not satisfied with making the patient

[1] Prologue, in *The Collected Works of Saint John of the Cross*, trans. Kieran Kavanaugh, O.C.D., and Otilio Rodriguez, O.C.D. (Washington, D.C.: ICS Publications, Institute of Carmelite Studies, 1979), 69.

aware of his deep motives in order to liberate him from the tyranny of the unconscious, thus leading him to take control of his actions in a reflective and resolute way. Here it is simply a question of changing one's life. The self-centered life must be exchanged for the you-centered one. "You alone are the Holy One, you alone are the Lord, you alone are the Most High, Jesus Christ" (the Gloria of the Mass). The old man is "homo incurvatus in se" (Saint Augustine): egocentric, closed, isolated, and fixed on himself. God created man to stand erect, to be free, receptive, and open. The Fall however, broke man's back, locked him within himself, and thereby cut him off from both God and his fellowman. In principle, Jesus has restored the original posture and rectified man, or rather given him an entirely new back, so that he has become once again *homo erectus*. It takes a long time, and the individual person suffers difficult trials before this principle becomes a concrete reality.

It is always painful to resist old ingrained habits. But here it is a question of much more: we must abandon ourselves, be willing to die. It is not a question of merely cleaning the house or fixing up the façade; rather, it is a matter of accepting the fact that the whole house must fall to the ground. The great breakthrough comes only when we completely accept the death of the old personality.

The fear of death is deeply rooted in us. Saint John of the Cross describes how desperately we fight against it as soon as God takes our prayers about being purified seriously:

> There are many who desire to advance and persistently beseech God to bring them to this state of perfection. Yet when God wills to conduct them through the initial trials and mortifications, as is necessary, they are unwilling to suffer them, and they shun them, flee from the narrow road of life, and seek the broad road of their own consolation, which is that of their own perdition; thus they do not allow God to begin to grant their petition. They are like useless containers, for although they desire to reach the state of the perfect, they do not want to be guided by the path of trials which leads to it. They hardly even begin to walk along this road by submitting to what is least, that is, to ordinary sufferings.[2]

Mary's Dark Night

Mary was without sin and had no need of purification. Nothing needed to be restored in her, since nothing had been destroyed. According to the Gospel, she nevertheless underwent a dark night. We can even follow her journey in the darkness step by step. The Gospels expressly name five "road marks".[3] We have already

---

[2] *Living Flame of Love*, stanza 2, 27, in *Collected Works of Saint John of the Cross*, 604–5.

[3] Cf. Hans Urs von Balthasar, *Theo-Drama: Theological Dramatic Theory*, vol. 3, *The Dramatis Personae: The Person in Christ*, trans. Graham Harrison (San Francisco: Ignatius Press, 1992), 330.

come across a few of them. It begins with the scene in Jerusalem when the twelve-year-old Jesus gives his anguished Mother the mysterious answer: "How is it that you sought me? Did you not know that I must be in my Father's house?" (Lk 2:49). Saint Luke adds that Mary "did not understand the saying which he spoke" (v. 50). His answer "explains" nothing for her. It gives her no light. When she returns from Jerusalem, she goes into a dark night, despite the fact that she now has Jesus with her.

Another road mark is described by Saint John. When Mary points out at Cana that there is no more wine, she receives the answer: "O woman, what have you to do with me?" (2:4). Exegetes and theologians have tried to soften these words and put forward far-fetched explanations. But we have no need of such explanations when we realize that Jesus is in the process of teaching his Mother and preparing her for a new mission.

When Mary attempts to speak with Jesus, who is surrounded by a large crowd of people, she is turned away. Those who thought that the Mother of Jesus had a privileged position now hear that his Mother is everyone who does the will of God. We will return to this scene, which is mentioned in the three Synoptic Gospels.

The fourth road mark is described only by Saint Luke. While Jesus is speaking to the people, he is suddenly interrupted by a woman who cries: "Blessed is the womb that bore you and the breasts that you

sucked!" A word of praise that the Church has repeated innumerable times in her Marian liturgies. But
Jesus does not seem to share the woman's enthusiasm:
"Blessed rather are those who hear the word of God
and keep it!" (Lk 11:27–28).

The darkness becomes a black night on Golgotha,
when Mary not only suffers with her Son in everything, but even experiences the Son voluntarily with-
drawing from her love and another son taking his place.
If Saint John of the Cross is right when he writes:
"the soul's greatest suffering in the trials of this night
is the anguish of thinking it has lost God",[4] then Mary
has truly experienced the most severe darkness of the
dark night. To lose God was for her to lose her Son.
When God is so close to someone that she can call
him "Son" (Lk 2:48), he cannot abandon her without
casting her into a loneliness, the depths of which we
cannot fathom.

"Who Is My Mother?"

It cannot be anything but painful for a mother who
wishes to speak with her son to hear him say: "Who
[is] my mother?" (Mk 3:33). Without a doubt, Mary
suffered from this answer, and even here Luke would
have been able to write: "She did not understand what
he meant" (cf. 2:50).

---

[4] *The Dark Night of the Soul* II, 13, 5, in *Collected Works of Saint
John of the Cross*, 358.

Let us first underline that Jesus did not say he did
not wish to see his Mother. Instead, he answered with
a question that burst the all too narrow perspective.
Jesus' answer often bypasses the question. In particular, in the Gospel of John, one is surprised again and
again that the replies of Jesus do not correspond to the
question. By giving an answer that is greater than the
question, Jesus wants to bring the question to a wider
vantage point. Every answer is a new challenge: Do
not be satisfied with such small questions, but, rather,
ask questions with a greater dimension. Instead of adjusting the answer to the question, Jesus awakens new
questions that are adjusted to his answers. The answer
gives more than the question contains and in this way
is an invitation to ask greater questions. So also Mary
is invited to the wider perspective by Jesus' answer.
She comes to Jesus as his Mother, and as such she
can be considered to have a certain priority with him.
But at once she is aware that she is not alone in being
his Mother. Mary, who at first stood alone, has now
become many. She is now a Mother among mothers.
But nevertheless, not in such a way that she disappears
in the crowd, as though she were only one of many.
Never has anyone done the will of God so radically and
without reserve as Mary. It is her absolute Yes at the
Annunciation that made the Incarnation possible. No
woman could ever be the "Mother" of Jesus if Mary
had not first given birth to him and given him to the
world. No person can say a Yes to God's will who has

not been included in Mary's all-embracing Yes from the beginning.

When Jesus asks: "Who is my Mother?", he does not disown his Mother but, instead, points out her incomparable fruitfulness. Her motherhood flows out and is shared by many others. "There is no purely private relationship between this Mother and this Son, only a catholic one", writes Adrienne von Speyr (1902–1967).[5] Catholic, meaning universal. Everyone is affected. Jesus is in the process of de-privatizing his Mother step by step and giving her a universal dimension. Without Mary's knowing it, she is being prepared for the mission that she will receive at the foot of the Cross, the mission of being the Mother not only of Jesus but of all mankind.

It is painful to be de-privatized. It always entails a death. No one has experienced it in a more painful way than Jesus. Everything became opened in him on the Cross, his hands, his feet, his heart, so that his life flowed out over the world. He, "the only-begotten Son" (Jn 1:18), by descending into our misery and death, became "the first-born among many brethren" (Rom 8:29). When he said to Mary: "Who is my mother?" and finally "Behold, your son!", he took her into his own destitution. He willed that where he was, there she would be also (Jn 17:24). Every new

[5] Adrienne von Speyr, *Mark: Meditations on the Gospel of Mark*, trans. Michelle K. Borras (San Francisco: Ignatius Press, 2012), 159.

distance he established between her and himself made her more like him, through a death that was like his death (Phil 3:10; Rom 6:5). It was precisely by being separated from Jesus that Mary followed him into that total destitution. "The visible humiliation conceals a hidden honoring."[6]

Star of the Sea

Mary suffered the dark night's deepest pain with Jesus, the pain of losing God, not because she needed purification of personal guilt, but because her universal mission demanded a break with all private relationships. Mary knew how it felt to lose him who constitutes the whole meaning of life. Because she herself went through the darkest of all nights, she became a star for all who would struggle with the dark night of faith on their journey toward God.

When we begin the ancient hymn "Hail, Star of the Sea", we greet Mary as a guiding star. She not only paved the way, but up to the last day she will continue to point out the direction. She is the flame that "shine(s) forth on earth, until the day of the Lord shall come, a sign of sure hope and solace to the people of God".[7] In a lyrical text, Saint Bernard of Clairvaux sings the praise of this star and encourages all who are in need to look toward it with unflagging trust:

[6] Von Balthasar, *Theo-Drama* 3:331n47.
[7] LG 68.

She is therefore that glorious star which arose from Jacob, and which cast its radiance over the whole world, the star whose splendour rejoices heaven, terrifies hell, and sheds its mild and beneficent influence on the poor exiles of earth. She is truly the Star which, being placed over this world's tempestuous sea, shines forth by the lustre of her merits and example.

O you who find yourself tossed about by the storms of life, turn not your eyes from the brightness of this Star, if you would not be overwhelmed by its boisterous waves. If the winds of temptations rise, if you fall among the rocks of tribulations, look up at the Star, call on Mary. If anger, covetousness, or other passions beat on the vessel of your soul, look up to Mary. If you begin to sink in the gulf of melancholy and despair, think on Mary. In dangers, in distress, in perplexities, think on Mary, call on Mary. Let her not depart from your lips, let her not depart from your heart, and, that you may win the suffrage of her prayers, never depart from the example of her life. Following her, you will never go astray; when you implore her aid, you will never yield to despair; thinking on her, you will not err; under her patronage you will never wander; beneath her protection you will not fear; she being your guide, you will not weary; if she be your propitious Star, you will arrive safely in the port.[8]

---

[8] *Sermons of Saint Bernard on Advent and Christmas, including the Famous Treatise on the Incarnation Called "Missus Est"*, trans. J. C. Hedley, O.S.B. (London: Washbourne; New York: Benziger, 1909), 46–47.

The Church also prays in the Litany of Loreto "Morning Star" ("Stella matutina" or "lucifer"). Mary made the original morning star fall from heaven (Is 14:12), and she herself took its place. She is the star that portends a new day. She turns our night into Easter night that passes over into an eternal day of Resurrection, a night when we can sing: "The night shall be as clear as the day" (the Exsultet of Easter night, cf. Ps 139:12).

Again we can ask: Is Jesus not enough? Yes, certainly. But it is easier when Mary is there. Saint Thérèse of Lisieux assures us that she also continued to perceive the presence of Mary during her severe trial of faith, when a wall reaching to the sky concealed heaven from her.[9] Saint Grignion de Montfort (1673–1716) writes: "In truth, there will still be great battles to wage and great difficulties to conquer; but this good Mother and Mistress remains so close and so ever present to her faithful servants, in order to illuminate them when they are in darkness, to elucidate them in their doubts, to strengthen them when they are fearful, to sustain them in their battles and difficulties, that in truth this virginal way of finding Jesus Christ is a way of roses and honey when compared to other ways."[10]

He explains further that love for Mary is not a means of avoiding suffering. To take up one's cross and follow the Master applies to all Christians (Lk 9:23). But

---

[9] Saint Thérèse of Lisieux, *Her Last Conversations* (Washington, D.C.: ICS Publications, 1977), 81.

[10] Saint Louis-Marie Grignion de Montfort, *True Devotion to Mary*, trans. Mark L. Jacobson (San Diego, Calif.: Aventine Press, 2007), 80.

Mary's presence helps us to bear the cross with a greater readiness. Her wholehearted Yes-attitude cannot but be contagious and influence the one who constantly looks to her. Grignion de Montfort dares to write that: "A person who desires to be devoted to and to live piously in Jesus Christ, and by consequence suffer persecution and carry his daily crosses, will never carry great crosses, or will carry them neither joyously nor to the end without a tender devotion to the Holy Virgin."[11]

Mary Mediates God's "Motherly" Love

There are several texts that emphasize God's "motherly" love, despite the fact that the Bible speaks of God as Father. "Can a woman forget her sucking child, that she should have no compassion on the son of her womb? Even these may forget, yet I will not forget" (Is 49:15). God's love acts "suaviter et fortiter" (gently and powerfully, cf. Wis 8:1 [Vulgate]). Sometimes it is predominantly the power we experience in love. Saint John of the Cross describes how love can cause the soul unbearable torments: "When eyes are sickly, impure and weak, they suffer pain if a bright light shines on them. The soul, because of its impurity, suffers immensely at the time this divine light truly assails it. When this pure light strikes in order to expel all impurity, a person feels so unclean and wretched that it seems God is against him and that he is against God."[12]

---

[11] Ibid., no. 81.
[12] *The Dark Night of the Soul* II, 5, 5, in *Collected Works of Saint John of the Cross*, 336.

When God's love reveals itself with such great power that it is experienced as wrath, just then it is very important that Mary mediates that gentle, motherly side of love. She does not contradict God at that time, but rather helps and encourages us to endure the weight of love. "Rest and be still!" (Jer 47:6), Mary says: "Humble yourselves therefore under the mighty hand of God" (1 Pet 5:6); he treats you in this way because he loves you. Mary does not show a different love from God's love, but she shows concretely that God loves us with a motherly tenderness. "You shall be carried upon her hip, and fondled upon her knees. As one whom his mother comforts, so I will comfort you" (Is 66:12–13).

14

The Marian Cult

"Placed by the grace of God, as God's Mother, next to her Son, and exalted above all angels and men, Mary intervened in the mysteries of Christ and is justly honored by a special cult in the Church",[1] says *Lumen Gentium*. At the same time, the council points out that the Marian cult, "although it is altogether singular", nevertheless "differs essentially from the cult of adoration which is offered to the Incarnate Word, as well to the Father and the Holy Spirit".[2] Moreover, theologians and preachers are encouraged to "abstain . . . from all gross exaggerations".[3]

It cannot be denied there have been exaggerations in the expression of Mary's great dignity. At times the thoughts surrounding Mary as the New Eve have caused the man-woman relationship to be pushed so far as to overlook the distance between Creator and creature. There has even at times been a quasi-divine omnipotence ascribed to Mary, based on the belief that Jesus was "obedient" to Mary not only on earth but

[1] *LG* 66.
[2] Ibid.
[3] Ibid., no. 67.

also in heaven. By doing this, one forgets that Mary's role in heaven is not to give orders to her Son but, rather, to pray to him for us. Some speak of a "merciful omnipotence" opposed to an omnipotence of "justice and wrath", which belongs to the Son. Others see Mary as a heavenly being who became human in order to give a body to God's Son. Still others consider her to be a co-creator of the world with God or as a complement to the Trinity. Saint Bernardine of Siena (1380–1444) does not hesitate to assure us that in certain respects Mary is greater than God!

Mary's Unique Position

Irritation over these kinds of extravagances could easily cause us to go to the other extreme and dismiss Mary from theology and the Christian life altogether. By doing so, we would be doing her, and most of all ourselves, a great injustice. For Mary *does* have a unique place in salvation history and in the Church. If we refuse her this place, we will lose something very important. "The Catholic Church," writes Pope Paul VI in *Marialis Cultus*,

> endowed with centuries of experience, recognizes in devotion to the Blessed Virgin a powerful aid for man as he strives for fulfillment. Contemplated in the episodes of the Gospels and in the reality which she already possesses in the City of God, the Blessed Virgin Mary offers a calm vision and a reassuring word to modern man, torn as he often is between anguish

and hope, defeated by the sense of his own limitations and assailed by limitless aspirations, troubled in his mind and divided in his heart, uncertain before the riddle of death, oppressed by loneliness while yearning for fellowship, a prey to boredom and disgust. She shows forth the victory of hope over anguish, of fellowship over solitude, of peace over anxiety, of joy and beauty over boredom and disgust, of eternal visions over earthly ones, of life over death.[4]

The danger with the Marian cult lies, not in the fact that one could love her "too much": when it comes to love, there is never "too much", one is always in debt (cf. Rom 13:8). "Have no fear of loving the Blessed Virgin *too much*," writes Saint Thérèse of Lisieux to her cousin Marie Guérin, "you will *never* love her enough, and Jesus will be pleased since the Blessed Virgin is His Mother."[5] As long as we allow Mary to be what she is, namely, the way to Jesus, there is no risk that she will take up too large a place in our lives. Through all eternity Mary will be the handmaid of the Lord and of his salvation. The problem can only arise if we sever the thread that binds her to Jesus and the Church and in this way take her to be what she is not. In God's world, no one lives for himself, but, rather, everyone defers to each other: Mary to Jesus, Jesus to the Father, the Father to the Son, and the Spirit to the Father and the Son.

[4] No. 57.
[5] *Letters of Saint Thérèse of Lisieux*, vol. 1, May 1889 (Washington, D.C.: ICS Publications, 1982), 569.

The Marian cult thus entails more than celebrating Mary's liturgical feasts. It consists, above all, in letting Mary become real in our lives, giving her the opportunity to be what she was intended to be. The celebration of feasts is meaningful only when it is an expression of an inner way of life and a means of deepening it.

This Marian way of life can be described in many ways. Inspired by the final doxology of the Eucharistic Prayer, one could say that Mary becomes real in a Christian's life when he lives "*through* her, *with* her and *in* her".

Through Mary

Mary was "exalted by the Lord as Queen of the universe".[6] To live through Mary is to recognize her as queen in our life. "I've made her Queen and Guardian of my heaven",[7] writes Blessed Elizabeth of the Trinity (1880–1906). Instead of deciding for ourselves what we will do, we leave the right to decide in Mary's hands. She is by far more clear-sighted than we are when it is a question of what will benefit us and what will harm us. She is God's living wisdom, because she was and remains totally at his disposal. When it is she who mediates the grace, nothing is distorted or corrupted. She has, besides this, the great gift of making

[6] LG 59.

[7] Elizabeth of the Trinity, *The Complete Works*, vol. 2: *Letters from Carmel*, trans. Anne Englund Nash (Washington, D.C.: ICS Publications, Institute of Carmelite Studies, 1995), L 298, p. 305.

the divine more human and adjusting it to our capacity.

"To be an instrument in her hands, to do only what she wills," writes Kolbe,[8] "one must allow her to raise us as she raised the Lord Jesus. . . . The Immaculate herself guides my pen and my spirit so that I will not waste time, ink or paper with useless things and so that I will not neglect anything she asks of me."[9] In practice, this means that during the course of the day we say "stop" now and then and take time to consult the "Mother of Good Counsel". For Saint Thérèse of Lisieux, it was natural to turn to Mary before she wrote the story of her life: "Before taking up my pen, I knelt before the statue of Mary. . . . I begged her to guide my hand that it trace no line displeasing to her."[10]

These small "consultations" both presuppose and create an attitude of inner peace and calm. Stress is an infallible sign that we are still going our own way and directing our life too much. "Let us surrender ourselves to her guidance," writes Kolbe, "let us be *calm, calm* and not try to do more or more quickly than she wills. We can let her carry us, she will think of everything, she will take care of all our needs of soul and

[8] *Entretiens spirituels inédits*, trans. and introduced by Abbé J.-F. Villepelée (Paris: Lethielleux, 1974), 38.

[9] Ibid., 62 and 89.

[10] *Story of a Soul, the Autobiography of Saint Thérèse of Lisieux*, trans. John Clarke, O.C.D., 2nd ed. (Washington, D.C.: ICS Publications, Institute of Carmelite Studies, 1976), 13.

body; let us give her every difficulty, every pain, and let us trust that she takes care of us better than we can ourselves. Therefore, *peace, peace*, much *peace*, thanks to an unlimited trust in her."[11]

To the one who objects that it is impossible to live always in this peace and that we cannot avoid often making mistakes, I wish to answer with Saint Thérèse of Lisieux that not even this should create a problem. What we have said or done wrong that cannot be repaired can be entrusted to Mary. We can be sure she understands the art of heavenly alchemy and is able to transform iron into gold. "The Blessed Virgin shows me she is not displeased with me," writes Saint Thérèse, "for she never fails to protect me as soon as I invoke her. If some disturbance overtakes me, some embarrassment, I turn very quickly to her and as the most tender of Mothers she always takes care of my interests."[12]

It would be naïve to believe Mary will show us exactly what to do every time we appeal to her. Since she mediates God's grace, which as a rule influences us from within, via our spiritual faculties, she exercises her influence in the same way on our understanding and our will, so that these become ever more attuned to God and we are inclined to make choices of love. As the handmaid of the Lord, Mary loves to make preparations and exhort us to obedience as she did at Cana.

---

[11] *Entretiens*, p. 95.
[12] Saint Thérèse of Lisieux, *Story of a Soul*, 243.

Her role consists, above all, in creating a greater receptivity. She knows that God will give as much as we can or desire to receive. That is why she does all she can to clear away all obstacles, so that we become total openness. Wherever she discovers the beginning of a Yes, she lets something of her absolute Yes slip in.

In Ignatian terminology, one could say Mary's most important gift is to create "indifference". Indifference is not the same as apathy. One could sooner call it a kind of "emptiness" that causes one not to feel more drawn to one thing than to another. One has no preferences, or, rather, one does not live in one's preferences. The one who is "indifferent" does not let himself be led by "I like—I don't like". What he likes or does not like is totally irrelevant to him. He feels a great flexibility and inner freedom. Because nothing is fixed, nothing decided beforehand, he lives in the breadth and length, depth and height spoken of by Saint Paul (cf. Eph 3:18). Every preference reduces his horizon and entails a limitation. If we distance ourselves from preferring one thing more than another, the horizon widens until it flows out into eternity. Indifference has something to do with poverty. One has nothing, one desires nothing, and therefore one has no need to defend or fear anything. The poor man is divinely free. He lives in a state of emptiness, and "when one starts from zero, everything becomes a plus" (Ylva Eggehorn).[13]

---

[13] *På marken, Bonniers* (Stockholm, 1974), 131.

Wind to Cushins

To bring out this "emptiness" in us is one of Mary's privileged tasks. She herself lives in it continually. She has always given the Spirit freedom to blow where he wills (cf. Jn 3:8). The Spirit has never found an obstacle in her. She is like an empty house with open windows and doors. She never knows exactly what awaits her, and she does not need to know. She already accepts everything beforehand. She has no will of her own, or, rather, it is her will that his will shall be done "on earth as it is in heaven".

When this fundamental Yes-attitude is present, we live in God's will, which does not exclude the possibility that we will continue to make many "mistakes", mistakes as they might seem in the eyes of men, but not for God, who has included them in his plan, so that everything works for the good (Rom 8:28).

With Mary

Mary is not only a mother who educates and gives good advice. We can also think of her as our eldest sister who shows us, by her life, how a Christian should live. In the family of Carmel, we have seen in her from the beginning a sister who embodies the ideal of the Order and inspires imitation merely by her being. Mary is a perfect example for every Christian. "They show her (the Blessed Virgin) to us as unapproachable," Saint Thérèse of Lisieux complains, a few months before her death, "but they should present her as imitable, bringing out her virtues, saying that she lived by faith just like ourselves, giving proofs of this from the Gospel.''[14]

When Saint Paul writes that we must be imitators of God (Eph 5:1), this can seem completely unattainable and, therefore, also nonbinding. And it is not completely without risks to imitate the saints, either: they all have their faults, and ''the devil comes to show their imperfections'' (Saint John of the Cross).[15] The one who seeks to imitate Mary, on the other hand, does not run any risk. She was completely free of sin from the beginning and at the same time human like us. While Christ is the ''sun of righteousness'' (Mal 4:2), Mary is the ''Mirror of Justice'' (Litany of Loreto). One of the mystics of Carmel, Maria Petyt (1623–1677), explains how it is wise not to wish to look directly at the sun but, instead, to see the sun reflected in the spotless mirror that is Mary. ''This mirror tempers the power of the rays and reflects them so that they adjust to our ability to see. In that way, one sees the sun clearly and distinctly, as though there were no intermediary between it and the eyes.''[16]

---

[14] Saint Thérèse of Lisieux, *Her Last Conversations*, (Washington, D.C.: ICS Publications, 1977), August 21, p. 161.

[15] ''Maxims and Counsels'' 78, in *The Collected Works of Saint John of the Cross*, trans. Kieran Kavanaugh, O.C.D., and Otilio Rodriguez, O.C.D. (Washington, D.C.: ICS Publications, Institute of Carmelite Studies, 1979), 679.

[16] *Maria a Sancta Teresia, vie mariale*, Fragments trans. from Flemish by Louis Van den Bossche (Bruges and Paris: Desclée de Brouwer, 1928), 31.

To live *with* Mary is thus to strive to act as Mary did, or as she would have acted had she found herself in the same situation. We take Mary as an example and norm and strive to act in the same way, so that there is no discrepancy between her and us. Mary was the first to live the way of the Beatitudes with total consistency. As our older sister, she has paved the way and shown the way of life we should choose when we belong to the Christian family. "Let us never say that we cannot," writes Kolbe, "for the Immaculate exists precisely so that each one shall be able."[17]

If we feel called to a life of prayer, we can save a lot of time if we are willing to learn how we should pray from Mary's example. The few words spoken by Mary that have been preserved make up a complete school of prayer. "Let it be to me according to your word", Mary replied at the Annunciation and, with these words, showed that she was completely at the service of God. The primary purpose with every form of prayer, meditation, or contemplation is to grow into Mary's openness, to let our body and soul become like Mary's body and soul: an open vessel containing God's life. Or expressed negatively: to grow away from one-selves, from all self-preoccupation and self-willfulness. The one who is in the school of prayer with Mary is not seeking spiritual "experiences". He is not seeking to realize himself through prayer. The only thing he wants is to become empty of everything that is

[17] *Entretiens*, 97.

his own in order to make room for God. When we choose Mary as a teacher in the art of prayer, we are more aware of all that hinders God's freedom and ties his hands. We discover better in what areas we are still serving ourselves instead of being "the handmaid of the Lord". To pray in the right way is always, consciously or unconsciously, to be like Mary, yes, even to be Mary.

The other prayer word of Mary preserved by Saint Luke is her *Magnificat*: "My soul magnifies the Lord." The more we make our own her "let it be to me according to your word", the more we experience that this first word of prayer changes into a prayer of thanksgiving. For when we abandon ourselves to God without reservation and place ourselves at his service, there comes a moment when God reveals his Son in us as he did in Mary (Gal 1:16). Then her "fiat" is transformed into a "magnificat". And can we do anything but praise God when we realize we are a living ciborium?

We hear Mary's third word of prayer at Cana, where she points out to Jesus that "they have no wine." It was said earlier that by doing this she teaches us something essential about intercessory prayer and shows us concretely how we should pray for ourselves and others.

These three words of prayer cover all of life's situations. The art of prayer "depends" on these three words.

One can also live *with* Mary when one reads the

Bible. She can teach us to read God's word as she taught Jesus to read it. She was, and is, well versed in the Scriptures, in particular in the Gospel, which is her own history. She can imprint in us her own reverence for the Word, which caused her to let the Word remain in its full power without always needing to understand (cf. Lk 2:50). But to read the Gospel with Mary means, above all, to see the word of Christ embodied in her. When we read that Jesus answers the scribe: "The first [commandment] is . . . you shall love the Lord your God with all your heart, and with all your soul, and with all your mind, and with all your strength" (Mk 12:29–30), we can let this abstract word become concrete by looking at Mary. She is the only one who consistently fulfilled the first commandment and kept all her strength for God. When Jesus spoke about the eyes as the body's lamp and pointed out that the whole body receives light if the eyes are healthy (Mt 6:22), it is again Mary who by her life proved the truth of these words. Her eyes were perfectly healthy, that is, continually turned toward God and his will, and therefore her whole personality was permeated with light. In every page of the Gospel we ought to attach an image of Mary and, thus, give flesh and blood to Jesus' words.

Mary can also be there when we celebrate the Eucharist. The Body of Jesus that we receive in the Eucharist was born of the Virgin Mary. She conceived it by the Holy Spirit, bore it and nourished it in her own body. The Eucharistic Body of Jesus does not deny its origin. The unity that has always existed between his Body and hers can never cease to be. That is why every Communion is also a remembrance of Mary's Yes, which caused the Word to become flesh. No one can prepare us to receive her Son better than she can. Saint Thérèse of Lisieux describes how she asked Mary to prepare the way for him: "I picture my soul as a piece of land and I beg the Blessed Virgin to remove from it any *rubbish* that would prevent it from being *free*; then I ask her to set up a huge tent worthy of *heaven*, adorning it with *her own* jewelry."[18]

In Mary

There is no life without a mother. To live in Mary is to know that one has a mother and that one is surrounded by her motherly love. She is the gate of heaven through which God's tenderness flows out over the world. Kolbe calls the Immaculata the "Incarnation of God's mercy".[19] Mary is so humble and transparent that she allows the divine to shine through without obscuring or minimizing it in the slightest way. Therefore, God can use her without risk in order to make his motherly love tangible and concrete. It is Mary's special charism to make the abstract concrete. Adrienne von Speyr says:

[18] Saint Thérèse of Lisieux, *Story of a Soul*, 172.
[19] *Entretiens*, 94.

Wherever the Mother appears in Christianity, everything abstract and distancing falls aside, all veils melt
away, and each soul is touched directly by the heavenly world. Mary, the purest being conceivable, mediates nothing of the heavenly truth without the co-
operation of the senses. What she saw and heard and
felt, what she experienced of the Child's movements
within her and at her breast, the whole palpability of
her Son's physical existence, lives on in what she reveals about him. She is a woman and grasps things as
a woman. In so doing she does not pull the sublime
down into a lower sphere; on the contrary, she has
the grace of letting what is distant from us become
understandable in sensible nearness.[20]

When we read the biographies of the saints, we notice that it is precisely the concrete they are looking for
in Mary. Thanks to her, God's love receives a "supple-
mental reality" for them. "You should take refuge in a
Mother's heart," writes Elizabeth of the Trinity, "the
heart of the Virgin."[21] When Saint Thérèse of Lisieux
speaks about the grace she received in the Magdalene
grotto, (in the monastery garden) that caused her to
carry out her work in the refectory for a whole week
"as though she did not do it", she sums up the experience with these simple words: "I was entirely hidden
under the Blessed Virgin's veil."[22] And when she had

---

[20] Adrienne von Speyr, *Handmaid of the Lord*, trans. E. A. Nelson
(San Francisco: Ignatius Press, 1985), 169.

[21] Elizabeth of the Trinity, *Letters from Carmel*, L 134, p. 63.

[22] Saint Thérèse of Lisieux, *Last Conversations*, July 11, p. 88.

such great pains during her sickness that she thought
she was on the verge of despair, she prayed to Mary
to take her head in her hands.[23] This image gave her
strength to endure a little bit more.

If Mary is our Mother, who shows us God's motherly love, it is natural to call upon her when we long to
experience this motherly love. Driven by a sure spiritual instinct, Christians have often sought help from
Mary in their need. She has been called upon as "comforter of the afflicted, help of the sick, refuge of sinners". If one reads the notes of Adrienne von Speyr's
visions (for many years she lived in familiar conversation with Mary and many saints), one sees that even in
heaven the saints have their small discussions. While
certain saints, for example Saint Ignatius of Loyola,
gladly advocate strong measures to get us lukewarm
and slow Christians finally to make a little progress,
Mary appears always as *advocata nostra*. She is always a
mother; she understands us, defends us, and gets the
more impatient and energetic saints to calm down.
Those who are shocked by this might consider that
different saints reflect God's many-faceted love in different ways, like the four evangelists, who, despite the
fact that they are all inspired by the Spirit, give us
different images of Jesus' personality and works. But
since Mary, of all the saints, has entered most deeply
into God's being, she shows him where he is most
truly God, namely, in his mercy.

[23] Ibid., 154.

Saint Thérèse had a refined sensitivity to the special role of Mary, while, at the same time, she was very aware that it was God who always has the last word. Three months before her death, she said to Mother Agnes: "I would, however, like to have a beautiful death to please you. I asked this from the Blessed Virgin. I didn't ask God for this because I want Him to do as He pleases. Asking the Blessed Virgin for something is not the same as asking God. She really knows what is to be done about my little desires, whether or not she must speak about them to God. So it is up to her to see that God is not forced to answer me, to allow Him to do everything He pleases."[24] If it happens that we do not receive what we ask for, there is no reason to be worried or disappointed: "When we pray to the Blessed Virgin and she doesn't answer, that's a sign she doesn't want to. Then it's better to leave her alone and not torment ourselves."[25] We cannot expect to be able to play Mary against God. Just as we cannot play the blue sky against the sun. It is just against the background of the blue sky that the sun receives its full splendor. If we pray for something that is against God's will, Mary will come and set the prayer right for us in a loving way. She helps us to change our attitude so that we begin to accept God's will.

To live in Mary is to dare to entrust oneself without reservation to her motherly and forming power. It is

[24] Ibid., 55.
[25] Ibid., 166.

not typical of her to do sensational things. She loves to work in hiddenness, to make use of the silence and peace of the night. That is why it is so important to entrust ourselves and our lives into her hands in the evening before we fall asleep. There is truly a great wisdom in the old Catholic custom of praying the rosary while we wait for sleep to come. While we are sleeping, we put up no resistance, and then Mary has the privileged opportunity of forming us as she formed Jesus in her womb, during the time she was expecting him. If we have our home *in sinu matris* (in the mother's womb) and give her full freedom to form us as she wills, we will necessarily gradually begin to show many similarities to Jesus. And we will then be children of the same Mother.

15

The Rosary

There is a rather widespread notion among non-Catholics that the rosary is a primitive prayer for simple souls to enjoy, but not suitable for people with an enlightened faith. In reality, it is a known fact that the rosary is prayed by people of every kind, by children, adults, lay people, learned theologians, beginners in the way of prayer, and great mystics. The rosary is such a fluid and flexible prayer that it can be adapted, without difficulty, to different people and situations. There are, in other words, many ways of praying the rosary. I would like to describe a few of these ways and by doing so to show what unimagined possibilities lie hidden in this simple prayer.

Vocal Prayer

The rosary is first of all a vocal prayer, and one can pray it as such. We pronounce the words and try to be conscious of what we are saying. We ponder the meaning of the words. The text itself is very rich. It consists of three parts. First, the angel's words of greeting to Mary in Nazareth: "Hail Mary, full of grace, the

Lord is with you." Then, Elizabeth's words to Mary, words that, according to Saint Luke, she cried out in a loud voice filled with the Holy Spirit: "Blessed are you among women, and blessed is the fruit of your womb." We who know the name of the fruit of her womb add: Jesus. Finally, there comes a prayer the Church addresses to Mary expressing her confidence that she, who is the Mother of God, will pray for us sinners, now and at the hour of our death. The Church reminds us that the present moment and the hour of our death have something to do with each other. The eternal dimension of the present moment comes into view in the light of death.

This wonderful text is always at our disposal. We do not need to look for beautiful words ourselves to express an inner prayerful disposition, which, moreover, is often nonexistent. No, we accept the prayerful words of the Church that, with the help, in part, of the words of the Gospel, teach us how to pray. Instead of stirring up subjective feelings, we enter into an objective prayer. We let ourselves be carried by the great prayer of the Church. We know that we are taken up into the great community of the Church; she who for centuries has prayed these very words.

Meditative Prayer

We can also pray the rosary as a meditative prayer. In reality, the rosary is intended mainly as a meditation on the great mysteries God has revealed to us and about which we read in the Gospels. Pope Pius XII called the rosary a synthesis of the entire Gospel. The fifteen mysteries of the rosary are partial mysteries, namely, fifteen different aspects or elements of the fundamental mystery, which according to Saint Paul is the folly of the Cross (1 Cor 1:18) and which consists in the truth that God became man and gave his life for us. "Though he was in the form of God, (he) did not count equality with God a thing to be grasped, but emptied himself, taking the form of a servant, being born in the likeness of men. And being found in human form he humbled himself and became obedient unto death, even death on a cross. Therefore God has highly exalted him and bestowed on him the name which is above every name" (Phil 2:6–9). We follow this descending and ascending movement when we pray the rosary. We do it together with Mary in her spirit and footsteps. With good reason the rosary has sometimes been called "the Gospel according to Mary". While we reflect on the five joyful and sorrowful mysteries, we follow God when he stooped down, ever deeper, even to the utmost humiliation, in order to be with him when he rises again and draws the whole world, and first of all Mary, with him when we meditate on the glorious mysteries. Since the disciple is not above his Master (Lk 6:40), and the servant shall be there where his Lord is (Jn 12:26), this double movement is not a historical fact concerning only God. It is also the movement of *our* lives. It is a life's program. Only if we are willing to accept our total incapacity can God exalt us and transform our human weakness into divine strength. Thus it is not only the life of Christ but also the mystery of our own lives that we deepen within us during the prayer of the rosary.

When we pray the first decade of the joyful mysteries of the rosary, for example, we can imagine Mary in Nazareth when she received a visit from the angel Gabriel. If we have a lively imagination, we can make the scene very concrete. We imagine Mary, who was perhaps praying, when she was suddenly surprised by the angel. It was morning or evening, or perhaps "night in its swift course was now half gone" (Wis 18:14). We are listeners to the dialogue that heaven carried on with earth and that was decisive for the destiny of the world. If we do not have much imagination, we can content ourselves with a general thought, for example, of Mary's openness and availability. We let her wholehearted "Yes, Father" influence our own inner disposition. We feel a mild obligation to stop rebelling against God and, finally, with an absolute Yes, place ourselves completely at God's disposal as Mary did.

Perhaps one wonders why we should pronounce the words when we nevertheless do not think of their meaning. In reality it is not as meaningless as it seems. Words have an enormously transforming effect. If we live with pure, positive, loving words, we are formed and stamped by these words, even if we do not continuously think about their meaning. Above all, words that have been recited with love by millions of people for centuries are in a very special way charged with meaning. We understand how non-Catholics can be shocked when they visit Lourdes and notice how carelessly and distractedly many pilgrims pray the rosary. But it would still be wrong to believe that such a prayer is meaningless or merely magic. Words are effective. Words have power. And besides, the words express and embody the will to turn oneself to God and open oneself to him.

Repetition of the words can be something that also engages the body while the thoughts and heart ponder the different mysteries. We are perhaps all too eager always to know and understand what we recite and pray. But through the centuries, even during nearly the entire history of the Western Church, the liturgical prayer was prayed in Latin. Many, we might say most, people understood very little of the texts of the Mass. In monasteries, the Liturgy of the Hours was sung in Latin. Perhaps it was not the ideal situation, but neither was it as absurd as many in our time claim. The two most important words in the Liturgy of the Hours are "Amen, Alleluia", and everyone understands these words. The essential thing is not so much that our reason, but that our heart is involved. And the heart often feels more free and can breathe more easily when the mind is not engaged.

Contemplative Prayer

Thirdly, one can pray the rosary contemplatively. One person feels a certain resistance to particular thoughts and images and would only wish to remain lovingly with Jesus and Mary, to love and let oneself be loved, to be together and feel secure in God and the Mother of mankind. The psychology of our day has much to say about the mother's role, about what it means to receive enough love from one's mother as a child. The Church has always known this. The rosary is a prayer where we give Mary the opportunity to be Mother, where we open ourselves to her gentle love. We reflected earlier in the book how Jesus said to his Mother on the Cross: "Behold, your son!" In John, all of mankind was entrusted to his Mother. Her motherhood received a universal dimension. In this solemn moment, each one of us received Mary as our Mother. The rosary helps us to let what we know with our reason sink down into our heart, to let it become a joy and strength in our life.

Intercession

A fourth possibility is to pray the rosary as an intercessory prayer for others. It can happen that one of our dear ones is in great need and asks us for prayer or that we think of the tragedies in the world: hunger, war, torture. We feel that we must do something. We can say: "O God, help these people, show your love!" But we feel such a prayer is too short, too cheap, that we cannot, after a few words, say "now I am finished." The rosary is a way of remaining in prayer to extend it. By praying a decade or a few decades, we show that we have taken the intercessory prayer seriously and are prepared to sacrifice time and energy for it. While we pronounce the words, we place the person for whom we are praying continuously in God's hands. We entrust him to his mercy. Can we do anything better for a brother or sister in need than to place them in the arms of Love?

The Prayer of Poverty

Finally, a fifth possibility. We can pray the rosary as a prayer of littleness and poverty. How often it happens that we feel tired, hopelessly distracted and totally empty! We feel we cannot concentrate and are too tired to pray interiorly or read beautiful prayers in a book. Then we can take the rosary and let our fingers slip over the beads while we repeat: "Hail Mary." Maybe our thoughts are flying here and there, perhaps many kinds of memories and images race through our minds, but we do the little we can. We give a little bit of our time to God, and we let our body, that willing servant, say beautiful words to God and to Mary, words about which we ourselves are too tired to think but which we know God understands. Certainly, we cannot be proud of such a prayer, but that is only an advantage. Many people place such great demands on their prayer that they never begin. God does not place such demands. I do not need to wait until I feel I am in good condition to pray. I do not need to make myself beautiful before I show myself to God. I may go to

God as I am. I can begin to pray now, immediately. The rosary gives the person who feels incapable of praying a chance to pray anyway.

We will have no excuse on the day of judgment when God asks us: "Why didn't you pray a little more during your life?" Many will come with the objection "I wasn't concentrated and relaxed enough to pray." "Oh!" I can imagine God answering, "Didn't you know about the rosary?"

Family Prayer

There was a time when it was a custom in a Catholic home to pray the rosary in the evening. I, who was able to take part in this, cannot but remember with great gratitude this common family prayer. It cannot be doubted that this daily rosary, prayed by the whole family gathered together in the evening, has been an immensely strong and unifying bond in many Christian homes and has, besides that, awakened many vocations to the priesthood and the religious life. In *Marialis Cultus*, Pope Paul VI insisted that this old custom should be revived. The pope was conscious that in our time it is more difficult than before to gather the family together in the evening. TV programs can be more attractive than the rosary. "There is no doubt of the difficulty. But it is characteristic of the Christian in his manner of life not to give in to circumstances but to overcome them, not to succumb but to make an effort. Families which want to live in full measure the vocation and spirituality proper to the Christian family must therefore devote all their energies to overcoming the pressures that hinder family gatherings and prayer in common."[1]

But if it is impossible to pray the rosary in the family, one may not use that as an excuse not to pray at all. One can also pray the rosary alone!

[1] No. 54.

Appendix 1

The Angelus

The Angel of the Lord announced to Mary, and she conceived of the Holy Spirit.

Hail Mary, full of grace, the Lord is with thee. Blessed art thou among women, and blessed is the fruit of thy womb, Jesus. Holy Mary, Mother of God, pray for us sinners, now and at the hour of our death. Amen.

Behold the handmaid of the Lord. Be it done to me according to your word.

Hail Mary full of grace . . .

And the Word was made Flesh, and dwelt among us.

Hail Mary, full of grace . . .

Let us pray: Pour forth we beseech thee, O Lord, thy grace into our hearts, that we, to whom the Incarnation of Christ thy Son was made known by the message of an angel, may by his Passion and Cross be brought to the glory of his Resurrection. Through the same Christ our Lord. Amen.

Appendix 2

The Mysteries of the Rosary

The whole rosary consists of fifteen so-called "decades" [Now there are twenty mysteries. Father Stinissen was writing this book before the Mysteries of Light were added by Pope Saint John Paul II]. One usually prays only five decades at a time, however. In each decade, we pray the following prayer ten times:

> Hail Mary, full of grace, the Lord is with thee. Blessed art thou among women, and blessed is the fruit of thy womb, Jesus. Holy Mary, Mother of God, pray for us sinners, now and at the hour of our death. Amen.

The decade begins with the Our Father and ends with "Glory be to the Father and to the Son and to the Holy Spirit, as it was in the beginning, is now and ever shall be, world without end. Amen."

For each decade there is a "mystery".

The Joyful Mysteries

1. The Annunciation
2. The Visitation of Mary to Elizabeth

3. The Birth of Jesus
4. The Presentation of Jesus in the Temple
5. The Finding of Jesus in the Temple

The Sorrowful Mysteries

1. The Agony in the Garden
2. The Scourging at the Pillar
3. The Crowning with Thorns
4. Jesus Carries His Cross
5. The Crucifixion

The Glorious Mysteries

1. The Resurrection
2. The Ascension of Jesus into Heaven
3. The Descent of the Holy Spirit
4. The Assumption of Mary into Heaven
5. The Coronation of Mary, Queen of Heaven

The Mysteries of Light

1. The Baptism of the Lord
2. The Wedding of Cana
3. The Proclamation of the Kingdom
4. The Transfiguration
5. The Institution of the Eucharist